Cromosys Publication

THE PLUNDERING PROPHET

NIRANJAN JHA SHOWMAN

Founder - Niranjan Jha Showman

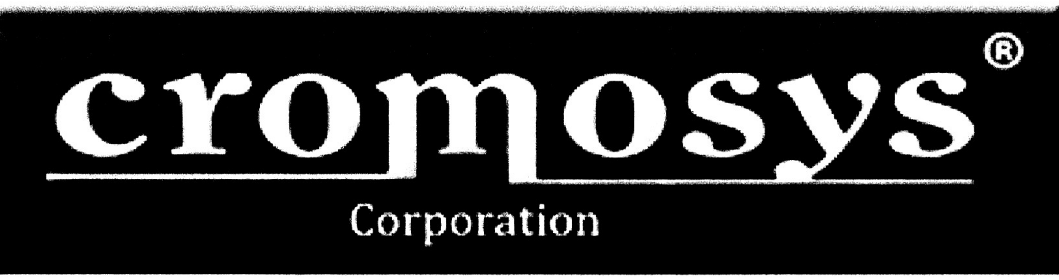

Education and Technology Research Center

Patankar Park, Nallasopara (W), Mumbai. +91-9561450045

Education, Technology, Publication, Healthcare, Newsmedia, Realtor, Filmmaking

www.facebook.com/cromosys

+91-9561450045
Learn Advanced Skills
And Get Job Instantly
GERMAN
Python
FRENCH
C++
SPANISH
Java
ENGLISH
HTML5
RUSSIAN
CSS
JavaScript
Cromosys
Education and Technology Research Center
Nallasopara (W), Mumbai

Learn Web Programming
Demo-Class Free
HTML
CSS
React
JavaScript
Typescript
Bootstrap
Cromosys
20 Years of Experience
Nallasopara (W), Mumbai
+91 9561450045

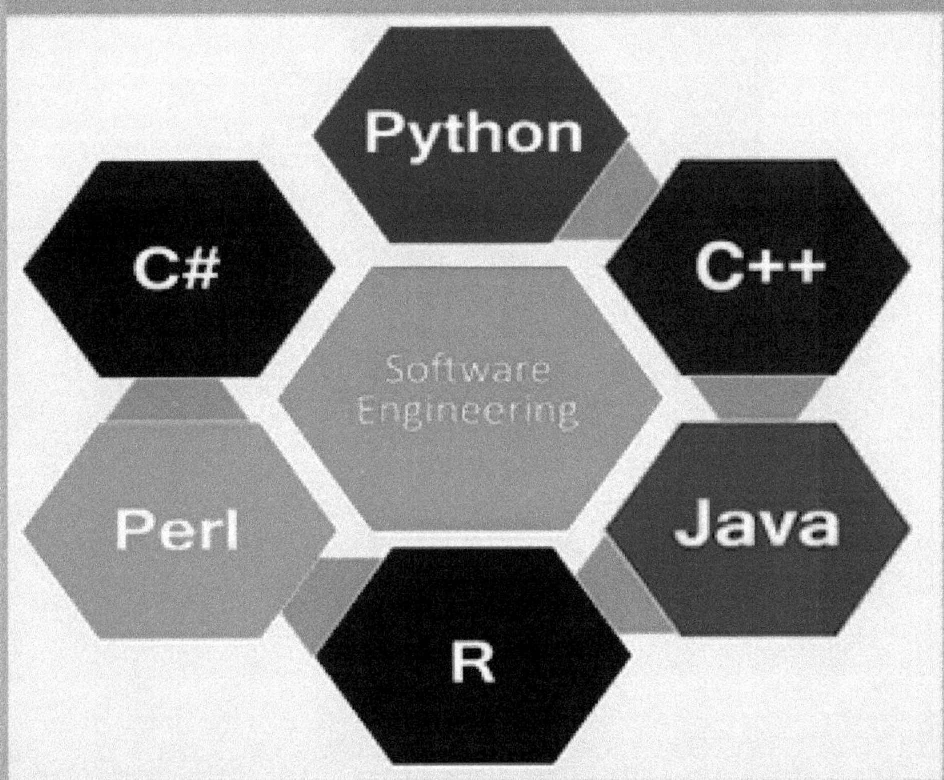

+91-9561450045
Learn Software Engineering
Demo-Class Free
Python
C#
C++
Software Engineering
Perl
Java
R
Cromosys
20 Years of Experience
Nallasopara (W), Mumbai
+91-9561450045

25 Years of Experience
Learn Visual Multimedia
Animation VFX
Movie Editing
Game Development
Cromosys
+91-9561450045
Education and Technology Research Center
Nallasopara (W), Mumbai
www.facebook.com/cromosys

Jobs Available
For Candidates Who Know

German

French

Spanish

Vacancy in Germany, France, Spain

For Hospitality, Engineering, IT Sector

With Free Visa, Airfare and Accommodation

Cromosys
Education and Technology Research Centre
Nallasopara (W), Mumbai
+91-9561450045
20 Years of Experience

+91-9561450045
Foreign Languages Institute
German, French, Spanish
Basic and Advanced - All Levels
3 x 6 = 18 Courses
FRANCHISE
Business Offer
Teaching Materials Provided
We have 1 Million Students Globally
Great Income Assured
Global Exposure
Cromosys
20 Years of Experience
Nallasopara (W), Mumbai
+91-9561450045

Cromosys Publication

The Plundering Prophet

Niranjan Jha Showman

"Love for God is good but intoxication for God begets crime."
~ niranjan showman

Preface

The early fight of Muslims from sixth century was for the conversion of Non-Muslims into Islam. And they succeeded in it on a big global bloodbath. But after this success, logically they should have stopped fighting but they didn't. They changed the mode of fighting and named it separatism as the new cause of war. It means separating their territories from Non-Muslim rulers and establishing their own rule. Even after succeeding in separatism at several places in the world, they are still fighting. They are still fighting even today. But this time, they Muslims are killing their own Muslims giving this mode of fight a new name – Caliphism. Caliphism means establishing their Caliph (king) rule in the entire world removing democracy from their own Islamic countries.

War between ISIS Khorasanis and Talibanis.
War between Talibanis and Afghans.
War between Afghans and Pakistanis.
War between Pakistanis and Indo-Muslims.

Why do wars in Islam never end? The so called prophet Muhammad ibn Abdullah established his religion Islam in the year 610 in Arabia. At the age of forty, he proclaimed himself a prophet, but while being a prophet, he indulged in plundering. Do you think a prophet should be and needs to be a robber? And when Muhammad was a plunderer, how his followers considered him a prophet? A diviner, proclaiming to be a God's messenger, proclaiming to have God's grace need not to rob others. His own power, if he had, should have played miracles. No other prophet on the earth has ever been a bandit. And if Muhammad hadn't been a robber, the world wouldn't have the terrorist organizations such as Al Quaeda, Talibanis, ISIS, Boko Haram, Janjaweed, and Hamas. We wouldn't have had crusade, Jerusalem crisis, and mass-forceful global conversion. Have they left the world any good to live in? And if these things germinated because of Muhammad's character, that clearly means, he was NOT a prophet.

About the Author

Niranjan Jha Showman
Trainer, Author, Physician, Entrepreneur, Filmmaker, Activist

Niranjan Jha Showman is a Language Scientist and Technical Researcher. He is the Award Winning author of more than fifty educational and fictional books at Amazon. He is one of the great-grandsons of the first President of India Dr. Rajendra Prasad. He is a Public Figure, and the globally - renowned Languages Trainer of French, Spanish, and German from past twenty years. Niranjan Jha Showman is an Entrepreneur and also works as a Filmmaker in India. Being the founder and owner of Cromosys Corporation - a company located in Mumbai, India, his company is excelling in the fields of Education, Technology, Publication, Newsmedia, Realtors, Banking, and Cinemascope from past fifteen years.

Niranjan Jha Showman's good-seller educational books and novels are appreciated worldwide. He has more than one million eBook buyers online, and more than one million learners are connected to him globally. One of his novels is critically acclaimed. He is the trainer of French, Spanish, German, English Voice and Accent, and Advanced Computer Education. He is also a political activist in India.

Niranjan Jha Showman is the man who came from rags to riches, he who knows how to turn the table, and he, whom you call the man of Midas-touch. He has observed lives from the Pandora of monkeys to the sanctuary of monks, not only down-to-earth but down-to-grave. He is a B. Com. graduate, and B. Ed. from Delhi University, and diploma holder in French, Spanish and German from America. You can watch his songs, movies, educational videos and many more things by typing "Niranjan Jha Showman" in Google.

Niranjan Jha Showman
+91-9561450045
cromosys@yahoo.com
Mumbai, India
facebook.com/cromosys

Statutory

This book with its content is the registered property of the author Niranjan Showman.
The author and his Cromosys Publication holds all necessary rights of this book.
The author does not claim this book to be true or untrue.

All the writing works that include all the educational, non-educational books, novels, and articles of the writer Niranjan Jha Showman, are the registered content under MAHENG12112/13/1/2009-TC and the endorsement no. 3244 28/5/2009 with the Ministry of Information and Broadcasting, Govt. of India. Any plagiarism in this regard will attract strict legal action. Any further publication or production of any of his books requires his written permission. The copyright certificate is attached at the end of this book.

Chapter 1
Muhammad stole Judaism and Christianity

Muhammad was born in Hubalism religion, a polytheistic pre-Islamic religion in Arabia. Before his birth, Judaism and Christianity had already reached Arabia but were spreading slow among the barbarous Arabs. Coming from monarchial Hubalist (worshiper of Hubal as prime God) Quraish family, he learnt at early age that his idolatrous religion Hubalism is much like paganism. Getting support from his first wife Khadijah, an affluent and powerful woman, he inverted Judeo-Christianity to form Islam which was quite favorable, supportive, and unifying to his mainland Arabia, the Arabia which Muhammad saw as a precarious territory in the fifth century.

Struggling tremendously, learning Torah and Bible, he conceptualized Islam – a monotheistic religion – based on the preaching of Abraham. Revolting against Hubalism, his own kith and kin, fighting and winning lethal wars, he established Islam on the rationality of monotheism. But this is also true that Judaism and Christianity, also having the same Abrahamic birth-source, which were already in the surrounding before Islam, were and are also monotheistic religions. The Islamic proclamation that, "If you believe in one God, you are the part of Islam", falsifies here because Judeo-Christianity were already believing in one God. And when they were believing in one God, Muhammad shouldn't have brutally persecuted them. The global persecution led by him clearly means it wasn't for religion but for power and wealth hunting. He wanted to establish and empire, not any God's kingdom.

From a modern Western perspective, the person, language and religion associated with Muhammad may often be viewed as obtuse, unfamiliar and even intimidating. What if there were bridges of understanding that would allow a seeker to relate to a common ground that is relatable? The purpose of this research endeavor is to ask questions from our Western religious perspective that aim to illuminate commonalities we may share with Muhammad. Casual readers of the Quran will quickly see that there are common themes, narratives and characters that originate in the scriptures of the Jewish and Christian world. So what is Muhammad's relation to these?

In prehistoric times, the primitive humans called Hominini were living in the forest of Africa. These Hominini, as the process of evolution, came out of the African forest and spread on the earth forming six civilizations – Mesopotamian, Egyptian, Indus, Chinese, Mexican and Peru. The Mesopotamians, in third millennium BC, formed their polytheistic religion which is called Sumerian religion – the first human religion on the earth. During the same period, a faction of Hominini, far later called Semitic people headed to new lands from Mesopotamia. The second faction of Semitic people headed to Arabian Peninsula to settle permanently while the first faction had already headed to Eurasia leaving Mesopotamia of low human density.

The second faction of Semitic people, after settling in Arabia (also called Bedouin tribes), became Arabs and formed their polytheistic religion Hubalism denoting Hubal as their prime God – much similar to Sumerian religion. In 2000 BC, they built Kaaba in Mecca. And the other faction of Bedouin tribes settled in Egypt and formed Kemetism religion. But the first faction of Semitic people (pre-Eurasians) spread as (1) Aryans – then in Turkey later India – religion Aryanism, (2) Romans – religion Mithraism, (3) Persians – religion Zoroastrianism, and (4) Israelites – religion Judaism. And Judaism was and is credited as the first monotheistic religion on the earth which was copied in Christianity and later in Islam. Now we will talk about Pre-Islamic Hubalist Arabs and their living style in Arabia.

Pre-Islamic Arabs were following either Hubalism, Judaism or Christianity. The big community of Hubalist were in the state of religious doldrums. Muhammad saw this as an opportunity and also a need to establish a new religion that could sweep the mass of Judeo-Christianity. Copying a lot from Judeo-Christianity, he established Islam, and so in early days of Islam, Muslims faced in the general direction of Jerusalem (not Kaaba) as the qibla in their prayers. And it was because of their soft concern to Judaism. After decades, they changed the direction to face the Kaaba, which was believed by Muslims to be a result of a Quranic verse revelation to Muhammad. When Muhammad had considered Jerusalem as the praying direction, what made him later revolt and exterminate Jews in Arabia?

Judaism is an Abrahamic, monotheistic, and ethnic religion comprising the collective religious, cultural, and legal tradition and civilization of the Jewish people. It has its roots as an organized religion in the Middle East during the Bronze Age. Some scholars argue that modern Judaism evolved from Yahwism, the religion of ancient Israel and Judah, by the late 6th century BC, and is thus considered to be one of the oldest monotheistic religions. Judaism is considered by religious Jews to be the expression of the covenant that God established with the Israelites, their ancestors. It encompasses a wide body of texts, practices, theological positions, and forms of organization.

The Torah (holy book), as it is commonly understood by Jews, is part of the larger text known as the Tanakh. The Tanakh is also known to secular scholars of religion as the Hebrew Bible, and to Christians as the "Old Testament". The Hebrew word torah can mean "teaching", although "Torah" can also be used as a general term that refers to any Jewish text that expands or elaborates on the original Five Books of Moses. Representing the core of the Jewish spiritual and religious tradition, the Torah is a term and a set of teachings that are explicitly self-positioned as encompassing at least seventy, and potentially infinite, facets and interpretations. Judaism's texts, traditions, and values strongly influenced later Abrahamic religions, including Christianity and Islam.

Let's look at the similarity between Judaism and Islam by reading this passage. Torah was called the holy book of Jews, and Quran was proclaimed the holy book of Muslims. Torah means teaching, and Quran literally means "Read That". Moses said that God revealed commandments to him on Mount Sinai located in Egypt and Israel. And Muhammad said that he received divine instructions on Mount Hira located in Arabia. Now you can understand the similarity between the formation of Judaism and Islam and see how things are copied from Judaism into Islam.

Some modern branches of Judaism such as Humanistic Judaism may be considered secular or nontheistic. Today, the largest Jewish religious movements are Orthodox Judaism (Haredi Judaism and Modern Orthodox Judaism), Conservative Judaism, and Reform Judaism. Major sources of difference between these groups are their approaches to halakha (Jewish law), the authority of their tradition, and the significance of the State of Israel. Orthodox Judaism maintains that the Torah and halakha are divine in origin, eternal and unalterable, and that they should be strictly followed. Conservative and Reform Judaism are more liberal, with Conservative Judaism generally promoting a more traditionalist interpretation of Judaism's requirements than Reform Judaism. A typical Reform position is that halakha should be viewed as a set of general guidelines rather than as a set of restrictions and obligations whose observance is required of all Jews. From this point onwards, you can also view why Judaism, not being reformed to attract mass, gave unwilling birth to Christianity and Islam after a big evolutionary period of time. And this is the reason that downsized the most prospering Jews community to become the victim of Christian and Islamic persecution such as Spanish expulsion, Ottoman brutality and – Adolf Hitler.

Jews are bound to hate Christians and Muslims the most. According to the Hebrew Bible, the United Monarchy was established under Saul and continued under King David and Solomon with its capital in Jerusalem. After Solomon's reign, the nation split into two kingdoms, the Kingdom of Israel (in the north) and the Kingdom of Judah (in the south). The Kingdom of Israel was destroyed around 720 BC, when it was conquered by the Neo-Assyrian Empire; many people were taken captive from the capital Samaria to Media and the Khabur River valley. The Kingdom of Judah continued as an independent state until it was conquered by Nebuchadnezzar II of the Neo-Babylonian Empire in 586 BC. The Babylonians destroyed Jerusalem and the First Temple, which was at the center of ancient Jewish worship. The Judeans were exiled to Babylon, in what is regarded as the first Jewish diaspora. Later, many of them returned to their homeland after the subsequent conquest of Babylon by the Persian Achaemenid Empire seventy years later, an event known as the Return to Zion. And this way, the Second Temple was constructed and old religious practices were resumed.

In 2019, the world Jewish population was estimated at about 14.7 million, or roughly 0.19% of the total world population. About 46.9% of all Jews reside in Israel and another 38.8% reside in the United States and Canada, with most of the remainder living in Europe, and other minority groups spread throughout Latin America, Asia, Africa, and Australia. In the flourishing time of Judaism, Jews were well spread all over the world and it was considered the most spreading community on the earth. Imagine, the religion that started in 6th century BC is now the very minor religion of the world. What went wrong or who wronged them? Judaism was first wronged by Christianity.

Chapter 2
Why Christianity wronged Judaism

Eurasia in olden days, before Common Era, was the hotspot of religious rivalry. Polytheistic Mithraism religion of Rome and Greece, polytheistic Kemetism religion of Egypt, and later revised monotheistic Judaism of Israel were in great conflicts with each other. They had to fight among themselves for superiority. For them, Aryanism (Hinduism) of India, Confuciusism of China, and Hubalism of Arabia were still far-fetched. Among the first three (Rome, Egypt, and Israel), Rome was the richest and more anxious to stop the expansion of Jews. Romans also knew that their polytheistic religion is going to collapse in the long run as compared to revised Judaism. Here in India too, Aryanism brought by Aryans wronged Dravidianism religions preserved by Dravidians.

This is the reason, powerful roman emperors with conceptualizers created the platform of Christianity and supported a new social code to grow. And this way, Christianity, the much revised form of Judaism, teaching detestation for Jews and Mithraite Romans, grew fast in and around Rome. The plain benignity of Jesus was glorified and replaced with divinity. Christianity gave big setbacks to Jews and this was the first reason Jews started leaving Israel with the hope to keep their religion intact in the other lands.

But it happened something opposite!

To understand what went wrong, let's first look at the basic structure of Judaism. In the strict sense, in Judaism, unlike Christianity and Islam, there are no fixed universally binding articles of faith, due to their incorporation into the liturgy. Scholars throughout Jewish history have proposed numerous formulations of Judaism's core tenets, all of which have met with criticism. The most popular formulation is Maimonides' thirteen principles of faith, developed in the 12th century. According to Maimonides, any Jew who rejects even one of these principles would be considered an apostate and a heretic. Jewish scholars have held points of view diverging in various ways from Maimonides' principles. Thus, within Reform Judaism only the first five principles are endorsed.

In modern times, Judaism lacks a centralized authority that would dictate an exact religious dogma. Because of this, many different variations on the basic beliefs are considered within the scope of Judaism. Even so, all Jewish religious movements are, to a greater or lesser extent, based on the principles of the Hebrew Bible and various commentaries such as the Talmud and Midrash. Judaism also universally recognizes the Biblical Covenant between God and the Patriarch Abraham as well as the additional aspects of the Covenant revealed to Moses, who is considered Judaism's greatest prophet. In the Mishnah, a core text of Rabbinic Judaism, acceptance of the Divine origins of this covenant is considered an essential aspect of Judaism and those who reject the Covenant forfeit their share in the World to Come. The origins of Judaism date back more than 3500 years. This religion is rooted in the ancient near eastern region of Canaan (which today constitutes Israel and the Palestinian territories). Judaism emerged from the beliefs and practices of the people known as "Israel". This religion traces its origins to the covenant God made with Abraham and his lineage—that God would make them a sacred people and give them a land.

Now here is what went wrong!

People of Canaan (Israel and Palestinian) living in social rivalry with Rome and Egypt surfaced their own religion Judaism considering it to be better than Mithraism religion of Rome and Kemetism religion of Egypt. Noah theory directly taking from the oldest Sumerian religion, Jews prepared Torah – the Old Testament. Even the Abrahamic theory in Torah is copied from Sumerian religion. Certainly, several of the stories which appear in the Old Testament, in particular those of the Torah which were written in Babylon, are either adaptations or contain elements taken from Mesopotamian myths — both Sumerian and later Akkadian religions precisely.

The unknown Jews scribes who wrote these stories were well-treated during the lifelong exile in Babylon. And in this exile they prepared their holy book. They were a valuable resource for their Babylonian captors, and apart from being well-educated, they had access to the ancient libraries in that city. It would have been from these that they gained their knowledge of the early myths of the region, which they incorporated into their works. Such copying and adaptation of earlier works was common at the time, and appeared to have been quite acceptable.

The Torah is the compilation of the first five books of the Hebrew Bible, namely the books of Genesis, Exodus, Leviticus, Numbers and Deuteronomy. In that sense, Torah means the same as Pentateuch or the Five Books of Moses. At times, however, the word Torah can also be used as a synonym for the whole of the Hebrew Bible or Tanakh, in which sense it includes not only the first five, but all 24 books of the Hebrew Bible. The word "Torah" in Hebrew means 'to guide' or 'to teach'. The meaning of the word is therefore "teaching", "doctrine", or "instruction". Jewish religious teachings throughout history, including the Mishnah, the Talmud, the Midrash and more, and the inaccurate rendering of Torah as "Law".

The earliest name for the first part of the Bible seems to have been "The Torah of Moses". This title, however, is found neither in the Torah itself, nor in the works of the pre-Exilic literary prophets. It appears in Joshua and Kings, but it cannot be said to refer there to the entire corpus (according to academic Bible criticism). In contrast, there is every likelihood that its use in the post-Exilic works was intended to be comprehensive. But after a millennium of good time, Judaism started facing criticism from Romans. Now Romans wanted to wrong Judaism as Jews had wronged Mithraism. Romans were planning to surface a much simpler and better monotheistic catholic religion than Jews'. Though by that time, Judaism had become monotheistic after modification. But Romans were persistent and the other reasons with Romans were to put a halt on expansion of Jews globally. Yes, because Jews at that time were spreading all around.

In the mid-2nd century CE, Christianity (formulated by Romans) began a gradual process of identity-formation that would lead to the creation of a separate, independent religion from Judaism. Christianity first developed in Judea in the mid-second century CE much supported by powerful Romans. Judea is a mountainous region in the southern part of the modern States of Palestine and Israel. And Christianity, based first on the teachings of Jesus and later on the writings and missionary work of Paul of Tarsus. Here, the plain personality of Jesus was glorified as the son of God. Paul of Tarsus, commonly known as Saint Paul, was a Christian apostle who spread the teachings of Jesus in the first-century world.

Initially, Christians became one of many groups of Jews found throughout the Roman Empire. The 2nd century CE experienced a change in the demographics, the introduction of institutional hierarchy, and the creation of Christian dogma. Jesus of Nazareth was a Jewish prophet who preached the imminent kingdom of God (the reign of the God of Israel on earth), which had been predicted in the books of the Jewish prophets. Here you can see the shadow of Judaism on the birth of Christianity. The Prophets claimed that God would intervene to restore Israel to its past glory in the final days. He would raise up a messiah figure (meaning "anointed one"), a descendent from King David to lead the movement. After a final battle and the defeat of the nations, there would be a resurrection of the dead, a final judgment, and God would restore the original plan (the Garden of Eden) for the righteous on earth. The wicked would be condemned to annihilation, Gehenna (the Jewish hell).

Do you think this preaching of Christianity is much different from Judaism? No, and why not, because the motive behind forming Christianity was to make Jews and Romans join this new religion. After the death of Jesus, his disciples began teaching his message in Jerusalem and the cities of the Eastern Mediterranean. An important caveat was added; belief in Jesus Christ would result in the resurrection of the individual to a blissful afterlife. With a Jewish message of redemption (described by scholars as 'apocalyptic'), the first missionaries approached Jewish synagogue communities that were established in the Hellenistic period. They would have encountered different groups of Jews who had their individual views of a messiah and the kingdom of God. We cannot verify the numbers, but apparently, some Jews accepted the claim that Jesus was their messiah, while the majority did not. And this gave a major blow to Judaism and left it as a minor religion shrink.

Chapter 3
Cursing Christianity Three Times a Day

As per the Christian book, the way Jews were called blameworthy of the death of Jesus, Jews became the subject of hate in the new Christian community. Even today, some Jews curse Christianity three times a day. Christian dispensationalists were early Zionists who continued to support Israel but not Judaism, for it is there that they believe Christ will return. In 1878, William Blackstone, a well-known dispensationalist and the author of Jesus Is Coming, wrote a document that argued for a Jewish state in Palestine. It appeared in 1891, five years before Theodor Herzl called for a Jewish state and six years before the first Zionist Congress. Blackstone got more than 400 dignitaries to sign his document, including the chief justice of the Supreme Court, the Speaker of the House, John D. Rockefeller, J. P. Morgan, and several other prominent Americans, almost all of them Christians. After President Benjamin Harrison ignored the petition, Blackstone tried again in 1916 with President Woodrow Wilson, who was more sympathetic—and who supported the British foreign minister, Arthur Balfour, a devout Protestant, when in 1917 he issued his famous declaration calling for a Jewish home in Palestine.

Can Jews and Christians truly reconcile?

The 1965 Vatican Council, and subsequent efforts by the Church to reconcile with Judaism, did not win over Orthodox Jews, who believe that their reading of the Scriptures is correct – not the Christians'. A new book discusses these uneasy relations. But it happened in Rome, in 1965. The Second Vatican Council published "Nostra aetate," a document in which the Catholic Church declared the abandonment of its anti-Jewish heritage and its desire to reconcile with Judaism. But the desire remained a desire only.

After the Jews were exonerated of the murder of Jesus, and after it was decided that they continued to be beloved by God, the questions then arose of why they had been punished by being exiled and of what reestablishment of a Jewish state signifies. If the Jews are still beloved, what is the validity of the ancient Church dogma asserting that "there is no salvation outside the Church"? Were the Jews exempted from this rule?

Christianity is rooted in Second Temple Judaism (second section), but the two religions diverged in the first centuries of the Christian Era. Christianity emphasizes correct belief (or orthodoxy), focusing on the New Covenant as mediated through Jesus Christ, as recorded in the New Testament. Judaism places emphasis on correct conduct (or orthopraxy), focusing on the Mosaic covenant, as recorded in the Torah and Talmud. Christians generally believe in individual salvation from sin through receiving Jesus Christ as their Lord and savior Son of God. Jews believe in individual and collective participation in an eternal dialogue with God through tradition, rituals, prayers and ethical actions. Christianity generally believes in a Triune God, one person of whom became human. Judaism emphasizes the Oneness of God and rejects the Christian concept of God in human form.

Judaism and Christianity share the Abrahamic heritage and are often referred to as being Abrahamic religions. In other words, they both claim descent from the practices of the ancient Israelites and the worship of the "God of Abraham". The primary figures of Israelite culture include the patriarchs Abraham, Isaac, Jacob, and the prophet Moses, who received God's Torah at Mount Sinai. Historically, Judaism went from being a religion practiced primarily in and around the lands that are modern Israel up to the year 70 CE to one practiced in lands beyond due to the exile and forced dispersal of Jews.

It also evolved from a religion centered in religious practice in the two great temples, to rabbinic Judaism and religious worship and education in synagogues. Rabbinic Judaism has been the mainstream form of Judaism since the 1st century. It is based on the belief that Moses received God's Torah in two forms; the Written Torah (Pentateuch) and an oral explanation, known as the Oral Torah, which Moses transmitted to the people. Judaism is a tradition grounded in the religious, ethical, and social laws as they are articulated in the Torah—the first five books of the Hebrew Bible. Jews refer to the Bible as the Tanakh, an acronym for the texts of the Torah, Prophets, and Writings. Other sacred texts include the Talmud and Midrash: the rabbinic, legal, and narrative interpretations of the Torah. Rabbinic Judaism is also based on the emergence of rabbi's as leaders, the study of the Torah, and thrice daily prayer.

Christians believe that God has established a New Covenant with people through Jesus, as recorded in the Gospels, Acts of the Apostles, Epistles, and other books collectively called the New Testament (the word testament attributed to Tertullian is commonly interchanged with the word covenant). For some Christians, such as Roman Catholics and Orthodox Christians, this New Covenant includes authoritative sacred traditions and canon law. Others, especially Protestants, reject the authority of such traditions and instead hold to the principle of sola scriptura, which accepts only the Bible itself as the final rule of faith and practice. Anglicans do not believe in sola scriptura. For them scripture is the longest leg of a 3-legged stool: scripture, tradition and reason. Scripture cannot stand on its own since it must be interpreted in the light of the Church's patristic teaching and ecumenical creeds. Additionally, some denominations include the "oral teachings of Jesus to the Apostles", which they believe have been handed down to this day by apostolic succession.

Christians refer to the biblical books about Jesus as the New Testament, and to the canon of Hebrew books as the Old Testament. Judaism does not accept the retronymic labeling of its sacred texts as the "Old Testament", and some Jews refer to the New Testament as the Christian Testament or Christian Bible. Judaism rejects all claims that the Christian New Covenant supersedes, abrogates, fulfills, or is the unfolding or consummation of the covenant expressed in the Written and Oral Torahs. Therefore, just as Christianity does not accept that Mosaic Law has any authority over Christians, Judaism does not accept that the New Testament has any religious authority over Jews.

Traditionally, both Judaism and Christianity believe in the God of Abraham, Isaac and Jacob, for Jews the God of the Tanakh, for Christians the God of the Old Testament, the creator of the universe. Judaism and major sects of Christianity reject the view that God is entirely immanent (see this as the concept of the Holy Ghost) and within the world as a physical presence, (although Christians believe in the incarnation of God). Both religions reject the view that God is entirely transcendent, and thus separate from the world, as the pre-Christian Greek Unknown God. Both religions reject atheism on one hand and polytheism on the other. Both religions agree that God shares both transcendent and immanent qualities. How these religions resolve this issue is where the religions differ. Christianity posits that God exists as a Trinity; in this view God exists as three distinct persons who share a single divine essence, or substance.

Can you believe in one fact that the Christian trinity concept is copied from Eurasian pagans? Yes, the trinity is a pagan concept. Throughout the ancient world, as far back as Babylonia, the worship of pagan gods grouped in threes, or triads, was common. This form of worship was also in Egypt, Greece, and Rome in the centuries before, during, and after Christ. And after the death of the apostles, such pagan beliefs began to invade Christianity.

Chapter 4
God based on sun theory

In Eurasia, the sun plays a major role in human life because of its cold region. Winter season is ominous to them because the sun moves toward the Southern Horizon (Winter Solstice) making the days shortened. December 21 marks the winter solstice when the northern hemisphere experiences the shortest day and the longest night of the year. On December 21, the sun stops moving southward, pauses, and then starts moving northward. This pause is called the "solstice," from the Latin words "sol" for "sun" and "sisto" for "stop."

In the Roman calendar, December 25 was reckoned as a good omen because the day begins to lengthen and the power of the sun starts to increase from that turning-point of the year. And this is why, on 25 December, their Gods are supposed to be born. Roman God Mithra (Sun-God) is believed to be a mediator between God and man, between the sky and the earth. It is said that Mithra (Sun) took birth in the Cave on December 25. It is also the belief that Mithra was born of a virgin. Zeus, the god of ancient Greek mythology was also born on the 25 December, and so Jesus Christ.

The cross has been widely recognized as a symbol of Christianity from an early period. However, the use of the cross as a religious symbol predates Christianity; in the ancient times it was a pagan religious symbol throughout Europe and western Asia. In paganism, the effigy of a man hanging on a cross was set up in the fields to protect the crops. It often appeared in conjunction with the female-genital circle or oval, to signify the sacred marriage, as in Egyptian amulet Nefer with male cross and female orb, considered as an amulet of blessedness, a charm of sexual harmony. And the same effigy appears on the Christian holy cross with Jesus on it. Pagans worshiped the sun on Sunday, so the Christians mediators having no fixed day to worship, took pagan's Sunday to worship and replaced their sun with Jesus.

The use of cross in the church began in the days of Constantine. Before Emperor Constantine legalized Christianity, the church was persecuted by the Roman Empire, and the cross was used as an instrument to execute the Christians. Under circumstances, it was nonsense if the church beautified the cross, which was a terrible instrument for the penalty of death, and used it as a symbol of Christianity. The church did not set up the cross for about 300 years after Jesus ascended until the time of Constantine.

There was a change after Constantine legalized Christianity. The church was rapidly secularized as a result of the preferential treatment of Christianity, and corrupt Roman Catholic leaders accepted pagan ideas and symbols in the name of evangelizing more pagans. The cross was one of them. They thought that the cross was a reminder of the crucifixion of Jesus to the converts who regarded the cross image as sacred, and so they brought the cross into church for them to worship.

Christianity did not destroy paganism; it adopted it. From Egypt came the ideas of a divine trinity. And in the book Egyptian Religion, Siegfried Morenz notes: "The trinity was a major preoccupation of Egyptian theologians. Three gods are combined and treated as a single being, addressed in the singular. In this way the spiritual force of Egyptian religion shows a direct link with Christian theology." In Alexandria, Egypt, churchmen of the late third and early fourth centuries, such as Athanasius, reflected this influence as they formulated ideas that led to the Trinity. In the preface to Edward Gibbon's History of Christianity, we read: "If Paganism was conquered by Christianity, it is equally true that Christianity was corrupted by Paganism. The pure Deism of the first Christians was changed, by the Church of Rome, into the incomprehensible dogma of the trinity. Many of the pagan tenets, invented by the Egyptians and idealized by Plato, were retained as being worthy of Christian belief."

So one side, denouncing Jews and on the other side converting pagans, Christianity became the strongest religion of the world. A Dictionary of Religious Knowledge notes that many say that the Trinity "is a corruption borrowed from the heathen religions, and engrafted on the Christian faith." And The Paganism in Our Christianity declares: "The origin of the Trinity is entirely pagan." That is why, in the Encyclopedia of Religion and Ethics, James Hastings wrote: "In Indian religion, we meet with the trinity group of Brahma, Viṣṇu and Shiva; and in Egyptian religion with the trinitarian group of Osiris, Isis, and Horus.

In those three there is one, and in that one there are three; the one God is indivisible, while the three persons are distinct and unconfused, God the Father, God the Son, and God the Holy Spirit. It teaches that God became especially immanent in physical form through the Incarnation of God the Son who was born as Jesus of Nazareth, who is believed to be at once fully God and fully human. There are denominations self-describing as Christian who question one or more of these doctrines. By contrast, Judaism sees God as a single entity, and views trinity as both incomprehensible and a violation of the Bible's teaching that God is one. It rejects the notion that Jesus or any other object or living being could be 'God', that God could have a literal 'son' in physical form or is divisible in any way, or that God could be made to be joined to the material world in such fashion. Although Judaism provides Jews with a word to label God's transcendence and immanence.

Paganism is a term first used in the fourth century by early Christians for people in the Roman Empire who practiced polytheism or ethnic religions other than Judaism. In the time of the Roman Empire, individuals fell into the pagan class either because they were increasingly rural and provincial relative to the Christian population, or because they were not milites Christi (soldiers of Christ). Alternative terms in Christian texts were hellene, gentile, and heathen. Ritual sacrifice was an integral part of ancient Graeco-Roman religion and was regarded as an indication of whether a person was pagan or Christian. Paganism has broadly connoted the "religion of the peasantry".

During and after the Middle Ages, the term paganism was applied to any non-Christian religion, and the term presumed a belief in false god(s). The origin of the application of the term pagan to polytheism is debated. In the 19th century, paganism was adopted as a self-descriptor by members of various artistic groups inspired by the ancient world. In the 20th century, it came to be applied as a self-descriptor by practitioners of Modern Paganism, Neopagan movements and Polytheistic Reconstructionist. Modern pagan traditions often incorporate beliefs or practices, such as nature worship, that are different from those in the largest world religions. Contemporary knowledge of old pagan religions and beliefs comes from several sources, including anthropological field research records, the evidence of archaeological artifacts, and the historical accounts of ancient writers regarding cultures known to Classical antiquity.

Jews were destroyed

The legal status of Christianity and Judaism differed within the Roman Empire: Because the practice of Judaism was restricted to the Jewish people and Jewish proselytes, its followers were generally exempt from following the obligations that were imposed on followers of other religions by the Roman imperial cult and since the reign of Julius Caesar, it enjoyed the status of a "licit religion", but occasional persecutions still occurred, for example in 19 Tiberius expelled the Jews from Rome, as Claudius did again in 49. Christianity however was not restricted to one people, and because Jewish Christians were excluded from the synagogue, they also lost the protected status that was granted to Judaism, even though that protection still had its limits.

From the reign of Nero onwards, who is said by Tacitus to have blamed the Great Fire of Rome on Christians, the practice of Christianity was criminalized and Christians were frequently persecuted, but the persecution differed from region to region. Comparably, Judaism suffered setbacks due to the Jewish-Roman wars, and these setbacks are remembered in the legacy of the Ten Martyrs. Robin Lane Fox traces the origin of much of the later hostility to this early period of persecution, when the Roman authorities commonly tested the faith of suspected Christians by forcing them to pay homage to the deified emperor. Jews were exempt from this requirement as long as they paid the Fiscus Judaicus (tax), and Christians (many or mostly of Jewish origin) would say that they were Jewish but refused to pay the tax. This had to be confirmed by the local Jewish authorities, who were likely to refuse to accept the Christians as fellow Jews, often leading to their execution. The Birkat haMinim (curse) was often brought forward as support for this charge that the Jews were responsible for the persecution of Christians in the Roman Empire.

In the 3rd century systematic persecution of Christians began and lasted until Constantine's conversion to Christianity. And when the Constantine era started, Christianity emerged gigantically defeating Judaism in all sense. And this defeat continued until Adolf Hitler's holocaust on Jews in Germany and Europe. And Jews lost everything forever on the silence of the pope during Hitler's brutality.

Chapter 5
Rise of Islam

The early 6th century pre-Islamic Arabia had Hubalism as the prime polytheistic religion denoting Hubal as the prime God. By this time, Hubalism was spread among sixty percent Arabs, ten percent were pagans, and in remaining thirty percent were Jews and Christians. Jews in Arabia were lurching in the lack of unity, and Christianity, newly arrived was meek to take big task of conversion in hand.

This was a great chance for someone to become the preacher and prophet in Arabia. Christianity was failing to spread fast in Arab world because neophyte Christian in Rome was sluggish in teaching Christianity to barbaric Arabs. This was the window through which Muhammad entered and surfaced Islam denouncing Hubalism, Judaism and Christianly – all three religions. The history of Islam concerns the political, social, economic, military, and cultural developments of the Islamic civilization. Most historians believe that Islam originated in Mecca and Medina at the start of the 7th century CE.

Muslims regard Islam as a return to the original faith of the Abrahamic prophets, such as Adam, Noah, Abraham, Moses, David, Solomon, and Jesus, with the submission (Islam) to the will of God. According to the traditional account, the Islamic prophet Muhammad began receiving what Muslims consider to be divine revelations in 610 CE, calling for submission to the one God, the expectation of the imminent Last Judgment, and caring for the poor and needy. Muhammad's message won over a handful of followers and was met with increasing opposition from Meccan notables Hubalists. In 622 CE, a few years after losing protection with the death of his influential uncle Abu Talib ibn Abd al-Muṭṭalib, Muhammad migrated to the city of Yathrib (now known as Medina).

The spread of Islam spans about 1,400 years. Muslim conquests following Muhammad's death led to the creation of the caliphates, occupying a vast geographical area; conversion to Islam was boosted by Arab Muslim forces conquering vast territories and building imperial structures over time. Most of the significant expansion occurred during the reign of the Rashidun from 632 to 661 CE, which was the reign of the first four successors of Muhammad. These early caliphates, coupled with Muslim economics and trading, the Islamic Golden Age, and the age of the Islamic gunpowder empires, resulted in Islam's spread outwards from Mecca towards the Indian, Atlantic, and Pacific Oceans and the creation of the Muslim world. Trade played an important role in the spread of Islam in several parts of the world, especially Indian traders in Southeast Asia.

Muslim dynasties were soon established and subsequent empires such as those of the Umayyads, Abbasids, Mamluks, Seljukids, and the Ayyubids were among some of the largest and most powerful in the world. The Ajuran and Adal Sultanates, and the wealthy Mali Empire, in North Africa, the Delhi, Deccan, and Bengal Sultanates, and Mughal and Durrani Empires, and Kingdom of Mysore and Nizam of Hyderabad in the Indian subcontinent, the Ghaznavids, Ghurids, Samanids in Persia, Timurids, and the Ottoman Empire in Anatolia significantly changed the course of history. The people of the Islamic world created numerous sophisticated centers of culture and science with far-reaching mercantile networks, travelers, scientists, hunters, mathematicians, physicians, and philosophers, all contributing to the Islamic Golden Age. The Timurid Renaissance and the Islamic expansion in South and East Asia fostered cosmopolitan and eclectic Muslim cultures in the Indian subcontinent, Malaysia, Indonesia and China.

As of 2016, there were 1.7 billion Muslims, with one out of four people in the world being Muslim, making Islam the second-largest religion. Out of children born from 2010 to 2015, 31% were Muslim and currently Islam is the world's fastest-growing major religion.

By the 8th century CE, the Umayyad Caliphate extended from Muslim Iberia in the west to the Indus River in the east. Polities such as those ruled by the Umayyad and Abbasid caliphates (in the Middle East and later in Spain and Southern Italy), the Fatimids, Seljuks, Ayyubids, and Mamluks were among the most influential powers in the world. Highly Persianized empires built by the Samanids, Ghaznavids, and Ghurids significantly contributed to technological and administrative developments. The Islamic Golden Age gave rise to many centers of culture and science and produced notable polymaths, astronomers, mathematicians, physicians, and philosophers during the Middle Ages.

By the early 13th century, the Delhi Sultanate conquered the northern Indian subcontinent, while Turkic dynasties like the Sultanate of Rum and Artuqids conquered much of Anatolia from the Byzantine Empire throughout the 11th and 12th centuries. In the 13th and 14th centuries, destructive Mongol invasions and those of Tamerlane (Timur) from the east, along with the loss of population due to the Black Death, greatly weakened the traditional centers of the Muslim world, stretching from Persia to Egypt, but saw the emergence of the Timurid Renaissance and major global economic powers such as the Mali Empire in West Africa and the Bengal Sultanate in South Asia. Following the deportation and enslavement of the Muslim Moors from the Emirate of Sicily and other Italian territories, the Islamic Iberia was gradually conquered by Christian forces during the Reconquista. Nonetheless, in the early modern period, the states of the Age of the Islamic Gunpowders—Ottoman Turkey, Mughal India, and Safavid Iran—emerged as world powers.

But something changed in the course of Islamic growth. During the 19th and early 20th centuries, most of the Muslim world fell under the influence or direct control of the European Great Powers. Their efforts to win independence and build modern nation-states over the course of the last two centuries continue to reverberate to the present day, as well as fuel conflict-zones in regions such as Palestine, Kashmir, Xinjiang, Chechnya, Central Africa, Bosnia, and Myanmar. The oil boom stabilized the Arab States of the Gulf Cooperation Council, making them the world's largest oil producers and exporters, which focus on capitalism, free trade, and tourism.

We have to agree to the fact that early Islam arose within the historical, social, political, economic, and religious context of Late Antiquity in the Middle East. The second half of the 6th century CE saw political disorder in the pre-Islamic Arabian Peninsula, and communication routes were no longer secure. Religious divisions played an important role in the crisis. Judaism became the dominant religion of the Himyarite Kingdom in Yemen after about 380 CE, while Christianity took root in the Persian Gulf. There was also a yearning for a more "spiritual form of religion", and "the choice of religion increasingly became an individual rather than a collective issue." While some Arabs were reluctant to convert to a foreign faith, those Abrahamic religions provided "the principal intellectual and spiritual reference points", and Jewish and Christian loanwords from Aramaic began to replace the old pagan vocabulary of Arabic throughout the peninsula. The Ḥanif, a group of monotheists that sought to separate themselves both from the foreign Abrahamic religions and the traditional Arab polytheism, were looking for a new religious worldview to replace the pre-Islamic Arabian religions, focusing on "the all-encompassing father god Allah whom they freely equated with the Jewish Yahweh and the Christian Jehovah." In their view, Mecca was originally dedicated to this monotheistic faith that they considered to be the one true religion, established by the patriarch Abraham.

According to the traditional account, the Islamic prophet Muhammad was born in Mecca around the year 570 CE. His family belonged to the Arab clan of Quraysh, which was the chief tribe of Mecca and a dominant force in western Arabia. To counter the effects of anarchy, they upheld the institution of "sacred months" when all violence was forbidden and travel was safe. The polytheistic Kaaba shrine in Mecca and the surrounding area was a popular pilgrimage destination, which had significant economic consequences for the renowned city.

Most likely Muhammad was intimately aware of Jewish belief and practices, and acquainted with the Ḥanif. Like the Ḥanif, Muhammad practiced Taḥannuth, spending time in seclusion at Mount Hira and turning away from paganism. When he was about 40 years old, he began receiving at Mount Hira what Muslims regard as divine revelations delivered through the angel Gabriel, which would later form the Quran. These inspirations urged him to proclaim a strict monotheistic faith, as the final expression of Biblical prophetism earlier codified in the sacred texts of Judaism and Christianity; to warn his compatriots of the impending Judgment Day; and to castigate social injustices of his city.

In Medina, where Muhammad was accepted as an arbitrator among the different communities of the city under the terms of the Constitution of Medina, Muhammad began to lay the foundations of the new Islamic society, with the help of new Quranic verses which provided guidance on matters of law and religious observance. The surahs of this period emphasized his place among the long line of Biblical prophets, but also differentiated the message of the Quran from the sacred texts of Christianity and Judaism. Armed conflict with the Arab Meccans and Jewish tribes of the Yathrib area soon broke out. After a series of military confrontations and political maneuvers, Muhammad was able to secure control of Mecca and allegiance of the Quraysh in 629 CE.

In the time remaining until his death in 632 CE, tribal chiefs across the Arabian peninsula entered into various agreements with him, some under terms of alliance, others acknowledging his claims of prophethood and agreeing to follow Islamic practices, including paying the alms levy to his government, which consisted of a number of deputies, an army of believers, and a public treasury. The real intentions of Muhammad regarding the spread of Islam, its political undertone, and his missionary activity during his lifetime are a contentious matter of debate, which has been extensively discussed both among Muslim scholars and Non-Muslim scholars within the academic field of Islamic studies. Various authors, Islamic activists, and historians of Islam have proposed several understandings of Muhammad's intent and ambitions regarding his religio-political mission in the context of the pre-Islamic Arabian society and the founding of his own religion.

Was it in Muhammad's mind to produce a world religion or did his interests lie mainly within the confines of his homeland? Was he solely an Arab nationalist—a political genius intent upon uniting the proliferation of tribal clans under the banner of a new religion—or was his vision a truly international one, encompassing a desire to produce a reformed humanity in the midst of a new world order? These questions are not without significance, for a number of the proponents of contemporary activity in the West trace their inspiration to the prophet himself, claiming that he initiated a worldwide missionary program in which they are the most recent participants. Despite the claims of these and other writers, it is difficult to prove that Muhammad intended to found a world-encompassing faith superseding the religions of Christianity and Judaism. His original aim appears to have been the establishment of a succinctly Arab brand of monotheism, as indicated by his many references to the Quran as an Arab book and by his accommodations to other monotheistic traditions

Chapter 6
The Plundering

The early fight of Muslims from sixth century was for the conversion of Non-Muslims into Islam. And they succeeded in it on a big global bloodbath. But after succeeding, logically they should have stopped fighting but they didn't. They changed the mode of fighting and named it separatism as the new cause of war. It means separating their territories from Non-Muslim rulers and establish Muslim rulers. Even after succeeding in separatism at several places in the world, they are still fighting. They are still fighting and fighting today. But this time, they Muslims are killing their own Muslims giving this mode of fight a new name – Caliphism. Caliphism means establishing their Caliph (king) rule in the entire world.

Islam teaches revolt more than any other religion of the world. It makes its male and female children hardcore adherent to Islamic faith by circumcision and female-genital mutilation. It strongly professes that Islam is the only true religion and others are bogus and punishable. It suggests conversion as a virtuous work and doesn't allow Muslims to live under non-Muslim rule whether monarchial or democratic. It doesn't praise much about nationhood, patriotism, democracy and cosmopolity but advocates much about Caliphism.

Because of religious inflexibility, Muslims are among the poorest of the poor in the world with around 40% of the population languishes in abject poverty – and not willing to change. For them, change is a sin because it will weaken their Islamic belief. Considering family planning also a sin, the poor Muslims' population are growing rapidly in Asia, and therefore even today, 30% of their children don't go to contemporary schools but study only religious books in mosques. When these pseudo-educated children grow, they don't get jobs. And when no job, becoming jihadi (religious fighter) is the only option. Centuries ago, starting from Mahommad Qasim, Mahmud Ghaznavi, Muhammad Ghori and so on, these invaders never let India live in peace. Learning from these aggressors, in current era, Kashmiri terrorists initially fought to forceful conversion of Hindus into Islam, and after conversion, now they are fighting for separatism. They spent generations in fighting only. Why so much of fighting and always fighting…?

Islam Spread by Sword

Kemetism founded in 6000 BC was wronged by Judaism and Jews became superior. Judaism, founded in 5000 BC was wronged by Christianity and Christians became superior. Christianity, founded in the beginning of CE was wronged by Islam and Muslims are trying to be superior. Islam, founded in 6th century CE was wronged by Bahaism in recent century. Judaism borrowed ideas from other ancient religions in the Middle East. For example, the Adam and Eve story and the Great Flood story in the Bible originated from ancient Sumerian mythology. The God in heaven and Satan in hell, originated from the Zoroastrian Religion which predates Judaism.

Historians describe Islam as one of the youngest of the world's major religions, having emerged only in the early 7th century CE. Within a century of Prophet Muhammad passing away, the early Muslims established an empire stretching from modern-day Spain in the west to India in the east. Many of the peoples who were conquered in this process eventually embraced Islam, laying the foundations for today's global Muslim community, which is widely regarded as the world's second-largest and fastest-growing religious group.

The tremendous numerical success of what European Christendom regarded as a 'wicked religion' has confounded observers for centuries. The only conceivable answer, in the minds of many, was (and is) that Islam must have initially spread through its inherent "bestial cruelty". From this perspective, the present day size and growth of the Muslim community is a product of episodes of history during which Islam was spread by the sword.

A key fact of this spread-by-the-sword narrative is the notion of forced conversions of non-Muslims to Islam. This is part of a constellation of questionable facts that have been repurposed many times in history. Of course, this narrative is not entirely unfounded. There have been certain instances in history of Muslims disregarding Islamic teachings and behaving cruelly toward non-Muslims, including cases of forced conversion, just as members of other groups have committed acts of evil (e.g., the Crusades, the Spanish Inquisition) that have contravened the principles of their own religion. Unscrupulous individuals and groups will seek to politically instrumentalize whatever ideology or faith they can, and every such event should be duly investigated and condemned. But to look at a cherry-picked selection of incidents and leap to the broad-sweeping, reductionist conclusion that Islam was "spread by the sword".

What was the reason of the success of Muhammad's empire? Muhammad's empire of faith has managed to thrive in the modern world for one simple reason: Muslims have kept Muhammad's dark past a secret. Indeed, they have gone beyond keeping it a secret; they have somehow convinced themselves (and many others) that Muhammad was an outstanding moral example, perhaps even the greatest moral example of all time. There are plenty of instances in Muhammad's life that one could view as the deeds of a moral individual, and Muslims are quick to point out his acts of charity and his dedication to prayer. However, in assessing the overall character of a man, we must take into account all of his actions, not just the ones that support our feelings about him.

If you ask the reality of Muhammad from Muslims, you never get the straight reply. A peculiar tactic is employed by Muslims whenever the character of Muhammad is challenged. When someone argues that Muhammad was a robber, Muslims suddenly cry out in one accord, "But he was merciful and kind! He started Islam, and Islam is good! God revealed the Qur'an through him! How dare you say something bad about him!? He was the greatest prophet ever! Stop being so intolerant!" The difficulty here is that, no matter how loudly a Muslim shouts these objections, they have no power to overcome the historical fact that Muhammad was a robber. Yet, to a Muslim who already believes that Muhammad was a prophet, the Islamic line of reasoning apparently makes sense. Nevertheless, to anyone who is not a committed Muslim, any claim to moral superiority will be an empirical issue, that is, a matter of examining and weighing the evidence.

Muhammad supported his fledgling religion by robbing people. The early Muslims could have maintained Islam through hard work, frugal spending, and the donations of admirers. Yet Muhammad chose robbery as his chief source of income, and greed soon became one of the primary factors in people's rapid conversion to Islam. Indeed, Muhammad deliberately used the spoils of war to lure people to Islam. When he was criticized for the way he distributed his newfound wealth, he replied, "Are you disturbed in mind because of the good things of this life by which I win over a people that they may become Muslims while I entrust you to your Islam?" Given the prospect of untold riches, it's no wonder so many people committed themselves to Islam. Muhammad guaranteed that Allah "will admit the struggler in His cause into paradise if he is killed, otherwise He will return him to his home safely with rewards and war booty." This message must have sounded extraordinary to the poor of Arabia. If they died in the cause of Allah, they would go to Paradise and be rich. If they survived, they would plunder their enemies and be rich. Either way, their situation would be much better upon embracing Islam.

Muhammad was often ruthless towards his adversaries. Punishments for taking a stand against Muhammad included torture and death. Both men and women were brutally killed for criticizing Muhammad. Hundreds of Jewish men were beheaded for standing against him, while their wives and children were sold into slavery. Some early Muslims who apostatized were killed after Muhammad gave the command to kill all who turned away from Islam. Modern Muslims often claim that Muhammad only killed when he was attacked by his enemies, but history shows that he murdered numerous people whose only crime was writing poems against him. Muhammad had far more wives than even his own revelations allowed. The Quran allows Muslims to have up to four wives: "And if you fear that you will not deal fairly with the orphans, marry women of your choice, two or three or four; but if you fear that you cannot deal justly (with so many), then one only, or (the captives) that your right hands possess". We know that Muhammad had at least thirteen wives during his life, and that he had at least nine wives at one time. Of course, he did receive a Quranic revelation telling him that he alone could exceed the four-wife limit: "O Prophet! We have made lawful unto you your wives whom you have paid their dowries, and those whom your right hand possesses of those whom Allah has given as spoils of war . . . a privilege for you only, not for the (rest of) believers". Nevertheless, since Muhammad was the one receiving revelations that allowed him to transgress rules that applied to everyone else, many people have concluded that he was inventing revelations to justify his hypocritical behavior.

Muhammad consummated a marriage to a nine-year-old girl. Muhammad's courtship of Aisha began when she was only six. Muhammad had a dream about her, which led him to believe that God wanted him to marry the young girl. Fortunately, Muhammad didn't have sex with her until she reached menses at the age of nine. Most girls do not have their first period by this age, but Aisha had been suffering from some form of intense sickness, which probably induced menses early. Muhammad apparently took Aisha's first menstruation as a sign that she was an adult ready for sexual relations, and Aisha quickly became his favorite wife. Among her earliest duties as Muhammad's wife was the task of washing semen stains off his clothes: "Aisha (may Allah be pleased with her) narrated: I used to wash the semen off the clothes of the Prophet (the blessing and peace of Allah be upon him) and even then I used to notice one or more spots on them."

Muhammad had a contemptible opinion of women. Muslim apologists often argue that Muhammad raised the status of women, and they are entirely correct in saying this. However, the status to which he raised them is almost as shameful as their status in pre-Islamic Arabia. According to Muhammad, women's minds are so deficient that the testimony of a woman is worth only half that of a man. Given this lack of intellectual ability, women have to be kept under control by other means. Thus the Quran sanctions the beating of women: "As for those [women] from whom you fear disloyalty, admonish them and banish them to beds apart, and beat them (lightly, without visible injury). Then if they obey you, seek not a way against them" (4:34). Notice the parenthetical remarks that the beating should be a light one.

We need to look deep into some more Arabic verses to understand the meaning of those verses. These words do not occur in the Arabic; apparently, even Muslim translators have a problem with this verse and do what they can to water it down. Notice also that the beating is done to bring the wives into submission. Muhammad repeatedly warned women about disrespecting their husbands: "The Prophet (the blessing and peace of Allah be upon him) said: 'I was shown the Hell-fire and that the majority of its dwellers were women who were thankless." Muhammad is unique among prophets in that he is the only one to receive a revelation, proclaim it as part of God's message to man, and later take it back, claiming that it was actually from Satan.

According to the earliest extant biography of Muhammad, he eventually became so sad about his countrymen's rejection of his prophethood that he began longing for some verses that would bring them to Islam. He soon received what he was looking for—a revelation saying that the intercession of three other gods was acceptable. Muhammad presented the revelation to the people, and his countrymen were overjoyed to hear that they could continue praying to al-Lat, al-Uzza, and Manat. But it got entirely changed after the conversion happened.

After a mass-conversion to Islam followed, but in time Muhammad received another revelation, which told him that the former verses had been given to him by Satan. God told him not to be too disturbed over the matter, for, according to the new revelation, all prophets occasionally receive ideas from Satan:

The apostle was bitterly grieved and was greatly in fear of God. So God sent down (a revelation), for He was merciful to him, comforting him and making light of the affair and telling him that every prophet and apostle before him desired as he desired and wanted what he wanted and Satan interjected something into his desires as he had on his tongue. So God annulled what Satan had suggested and God established His verses, i.e. you are just like the prophets and apostles. Then God sent down: "We have not sent a prophet or apostle before you but when he longed Satan cast suggestions in his longing. But God will annul what Satan has suggested. Then God will establish his verses, God being knowing and wise."

Chapter 7
Islamic terrorism

These are just some of the facts that Muslims have been keeping secret, but they are enough to make any reasonable person doubt the validity of Islam. Muhammad was guilty of countless murders and of torturing his victims. He robbed caravans and participated in the slave-trade. His persecution of the Jews bordered on genocide. His polygamy went beyond that which even his own revelations permitted (though he did receive a revelation saying that this was okay for him). One of his wives was a nine-year-old girl, whose earliest duties in Muhammad's house included the constant task of washing the semen stains off his clothes. At times he believed he was demon-possessed or under the effect of magic. He was known to be suicidal. He admittedly received a message from Satan and delivered it to the people as if it were from God. He declared that women have half the intellectual ability that men have, that it is okay for men to beat their wives, that most of the inhabitants of hell are women, and that, even if a woman somehow makes it to heaven, her eternity will consist of standing in a corner, waiting for men to sexually enjoy her.

These details about Muhammad raise a very important question: What does a prophet have to do before Muslims will be willing to question whether he is truly the greatest moral example in history? Normally, when we say that someone is a moral person, we mean that he doesn't commit acts such as robbery and murder. Yet Muhammad did all these things and much more. It appears, then, that Muslims are using the term "moral" in a very unique way. In this uniquely Muslim sense of the term, the word "moral" is defined as "whatever Muhammad does." Thus, if Muhammad were to chop off the heads of hundreds of people (which he did), this act would still be defined as a moral act, since Muhammad did it, and anything Muhammad does is, by definition, moral.

But this raises another important question. If God's greatest prophet is free to take part in murder, robbery, genocide, and slave-trading, can we really point a finger at people like Osama bin Laden and Saddam Hussein and say that they are evil? They killed many innocents, but so did Muhammad. Saddam tortured countless people, but so did Muhammad. In fact, one could make a case that Osama bin Laden is morally superior to Muhammad, for, while bin Laden killed thousands of people, he didn't sell their wives and children into slavery, or have sex with a little girl, or marry more than a dozen women.

The truth about Muhammad has been one of the world's best-kept secrets. For centuries, it has been virtually impossible to raise objections about the character of Muhammad in Muslim countries, for anyone who raised such objections would (following the example set by Muhammad himself) immediately be killed. Outside the Muslim world, there has been little interest in Islam, and those who have been interested have typically relied on modern Muslim reports about Muhammad, such as the above passage from Mawdudi. But things have changed. Now many people are interested in Islam, and Muslims aren't able to silence everyone. Moreover, with the advent of the Internet, it is now impossible to keep Muhammad's life a secret. The facts about the founder of Islam are spreading very rapidly, and Muslims are frantically scurrying to defend their faith. But the information superhighway is paving over the ignorance that has for centuries been the stronghold of Islamic dogma. In the end, Islam will fall, for the entire structure is built upon the belief that Muhammad was the greatest moral example in history, and this belief is demonstrably false.

In current time, Islamic terrorism also refers to terrorist acts with religious motivations carried out by fundamentalist militant groups. The September 11 attacks against the United States in 2001 were carried out by the Islamist terrorist group al-Qaeda. Incidents and fatalities from Islamic terrorism have been concentrated in eight Muslim-majority countries (Afghanistan, Egypt, Iraq, Libya, Nigeria, Pakistan, Somalia, and Syria), while four Islamic extremist groups (Islamic State, Boko Haram, the Taliban, and al-Qaeda) were responsible for 74% of all deaths from terrorism in 2015. The annual number of fatalities from terrorist attacks grew sharply from 2011 to 2014 when it reached a peak of 33,438, before declining to 13,826 in 2019.

Since at least the 1990s, these terrorist incidents have occurred on a global scale, affecting not only Muslim-majority countries in Africa and Asia, but also Russia, Australia, Canada, Israel, India, the United States, China, Philippines, Thailand and countries within Europe. Such attacks have targeted both Muslims and non-Muslims, with one study finding 80% of terrorist victims to be Muslims. In a number of the worst-affected Muslim-majority regions, these terrorists have been met by armed, independent resistance groups, state actors and their proxies, and elsewhere by condemnation by prominent Islamic figures. Journalists have also become targets of Islamic terrorism, particularly for the depiction of the Islamic prophet Muhammad, with the Charlie Hebdo shooting being protested by millions in France.

Justifications given for attacks on civilians by Islamic extremist and terrorist groups come from their interpretations of the Quran, the hadith, and sharia law. These include retribution by armed jihad for the perceived injustices of unbelievers against Muslims; the belief that the killing of many self-proclaimed Muslims is required because they have violated Islamic law and are disbelievers; the overriding necessity of restoring and purifying Islam by establishing sharia law, especially by restoring the Caliphate as a pan-Islamic state (especially ISIS); the glory and heavenly rewards of martyrdom; the supremacy of Islam over all other religions.

After failed attempts at state formation and the creation of Israel in the post-colonial era, a series of Marxist and anti-Western transformations and movements swept throughout the Arab and Islamic world. These movements were nationalist and revolutionary not Islamic, but their view that terrorism could be effective in reaching their political goals generated the first phase of modern international terrorism. In the late 1960s, Palestinian secular movements such as Al Fatah and the Popular Front for the Liberation of Palestine (PFLP) began to target civilians outside the immediate arena of conflict. Following Israel's 1967 defeat of Arab forces, Palestinian leaders began to see that the Arab world was unable to militarily confront Israel. During the same time, lessons drawn from revolutionary movements in Latin America, North Africa, Southeast Asia as well as during the Jewish struggle against Britain in Palestine, saw the Palestinians turn away from guerrilla warfare towards urban terrorism. These movements were secular in nature but their international organization served to spread terrorist tactics worldwide.

After the decisive defeat by Israel of Arab armies led by Arab nationalist regimes in the Six-Day War, religiously motivated/Islamic movements grew in the Middle East and came into conflict with secular nationalism. Islamic groups were supported by Saudi Arabia, to counter nationalist ideology. According to Bruce Hoffman of the RAND Corporation, in 1980, 2 out of 64 terrorist groups were categorized as having religious motivation while in 1995, almost half (26 out of 56) were religiously motivated with the majority having Islam as their guiding force.

While Islamic opponents of attacks on civilians have quoted numerous prophetic hadith and hadith by Muhammad's first successor Abu Bakr, Al-Qaeda believes its attacks are religiously justified. After its first attack on a US target that killed civilians instead (a 1992 bombing of a hotel in Aden Yemen), Al Qaeda justified the killing of civilian bystanders through an interpretation (by one Abu Hajer) based on medieval jurist Ibn Taymiyyah.

In a post 9/11 attack, a statement from Qaidat al-Jihad regarding the mandates of the heroes and the legality of the operations in New York and Washington, Al-Qaeda provided a more systematic justification—one that provided ample theological justification for killing civilians in almost any imaginable situation. Among these justifications are that America is leading the countries of the West in waging war on Islam, which (al-Qaeda alleges) targets "Muslim women, children and elderly". This means any attacks on America are a defense of Islam, and any treaties and agreements between Muslim majority states and Western countries that would be violated by attacks are null and void.

Their justification for killing is not without logic – but their own logic. Other justifications for killing and situations where killings is allowed based on precedents in early Islamic history include: killing non-combatants when it is too difficult to distinguish between them and combatants when attacking an enemy "stronghold" (hist), and/or non-combatants remain in enemy territory; killing those who assist the enemy "in deed, word, mind", this includes civilians since they can vote in elections that bring enemies of Islam to power; necessity of killing in the war to protect Islam and Muslims; when the prophet was asked whether Muslim fighters could use the catapult against the village of Taif, even though the enemy fighters were mixed with a civilian population, he indicated in the affirmative; killing women, children and other protected groups is allowed when they serve as human shields for the enemy; killing of civilians is permitted if the enemy has broken a treaty.

Supporters of bin Laden have pointed to reports according to which the Islamic prophet Muhammad attacked towns at night or with catapults, and argued that he must have condoned incidental harm to noncombatants, since it would have been impossible to distinguish them from combatants during such attacks. These arguments were not widely accepted by Muslims.

In the next chapters, we will read how the Islamic terrorist organizations such Al-Qaeda, Talibanis, ISIS, and TTP were formed and how they influenced human life in Muslim communities to fight against non-Muslims. It is not that the truth is horrible so we should not discuss, but you should know why it is horrible. Why fights never end in Islam? And why now Islam is against Islam?

Chapter 8
Islam against Islam

Islamic terrorist organizations such Al-Qaeda, Talibanis, ISIS, and TTP were formed as rebellion group against non-Muslim elements. But from past two decades, they are fighting among each other for power imposing a white lie – a lie of establishing Caliph Rule. And this brings democratic Islam against rebellious Islam – means Islam against Islam.

Al-Qaeda

In 1988, after Soviet forces were defeated and withdrew from Afghanistan, Osama bin Laden founded an aggressive organization called al Qaeda, or "the Base," to continue the cause of jihad (holy war) through violence and aggression and was founded in 1988, Peshawar, Pakistan. Al-Qaeda is a multinational militant Sunni Islamic extremist network composed of Salafist jihadists. Its members are mostly composed of Arabs, but may also include other peoples. Al-Qaeda has mounted attacks on non-military and military targets in various countries, including the 1998 United States embassy bombings, the September 11 attacks, and the 2002 Bali bombings; it has been designated as a terrorist group by the United Nations Security Council, the North Atlantic Treaty Organization (NATO), the European Union, India, and various other countries.

The network was founded in 1988 by Osama bin Laden, Abdullah Azzam, and other Arab volunteers during the Soviet–Afghan War. After fighting this war, the group aimed to expand such operations to other parts of the world, setting up bases in parts of Africa, the Arab world and elsewhere, carrying out many attacks on people whom it considers non-believers.

Al-Qaeda members believe a Christian-Jewish alliance (led by the United States) is conspiring to be at war against Islam and destroy Islam. As Salafist jihadists, members of al-Qaeda believe that killing non-combatants is religiously sanctioned. Al-Qaeda also opposes what it regards as man-made laws, and wants to replace them exclusively with a strict form of sharī'a (Islamic religious law, which is perceived as divine law). It is also responsible for instigating sectarian violence among Muslims. Al-Qaeda regards liberal Muslims, Shias, Sufis, and other Islamic sects as heretical and its members and sympathizers have attacked their mosques, shrines, and gatherings. Examples of sectarian attacks include the 2004 Ashoura massacre, the 2006 Sadr City bombings, the April 2007 Baghdad bombings, and the 2007 Yazidi community bombings. Islam against Islam!

The United States government responded to the September 11 attacks by launching the "war on terror", which sought to undermine al-Qaeda and its allies. The combined army operation of many US allied countries devastated this Islamic militant group. The deaths of key leaders, including that of Osama bin Laden, have led al-Qaeda's operations to shift from top-down organization and planning of attacks, to the planning of attacks carried out by a loose network of associated groups and lone-wolf operators. Al-Qaeda characteristically organizes attacks including suicide attacks and simultaneous bombing of several targets. Al-Qaeda ideologues envision the violent removal of all foreign and secular influences in Muslim countries, which it perceives as corrupt deviations. Following the death of Osama bin Laden in 2011, the group was led by Egyptian Ayman al-Zawahiri until his death in 2022. As of 2021, it has reportedly suffered from a deterioration of central command over its regional operations.

Talibanis and ISIS

As Islam was spread on sword, now its followers engage always in fight. The Islamic State (ISIS) and Taliban conflict is an ongoing armed conflict in Afghanistan. The conflict escalated when militants who were affiliated with IS-K killed Abdul Ghani, a senior Taliban commander in Logar province on 2 February 2015. Since then, Taliban and IS-K have engaged in clashes over the control of territory, mostly in eastern Afghanistan, but clashes have also occurred between the Taliban and ISIS-K cells which are located in the north-west and south-west.

The Haqqani network, Al-Qaeda and others support the Taliban, while IS is supported by the High Council of the Islamic Emirate of Afghanistan, the Mullah Dadullah Front and the pro-ISIS faction of the Islamic Movement of Uzbekistan. After the takeover of Kabul by the Taliban in 2021, several members of the Afghan intelligence agency and the Afghan national army have also joined the Islamic State – Khorasan Province. In February 2022, Pakistani officials acknowledged that ongoing violence was destabilizing the region and creating a problem for Pakistan.

During their original stint in power of the Islamic Emirate of Afghanistan in the late 1990s, the ruling Taliban had pursued a policy of suppressing Salafism; motivated by strict Deobandi tenets. During this period, the main issue of Salafist scholars was that Taliban was led by Maturidi Sufis. As a result of the unofficial Taliban bans on Ahl-i Hadith during the 1996-2001 era, several Salafis had shifted to Peshawar. However, after the US-led Invasion of Afghanistan in 2001, Taliban and Ahl-i Hadith allied to wage a common Jihad to resist the invasion. The Afghan Salafists decided to put aside their differences with the Taliban to join them in the "greater jihad" against the United States. Several Arab Salafis in Al-Qaeda rank and file would mediate the disputes between Afghan Salafists and Taliban; enabling them to unify for the more important religious duty of fighting against the U.S and its allies in Afghanistan. Many Salafi commanders and Ahl-i Hadith organizations participated in the Taliban insurgency (2001-2021) under Afghan Taliban's command.

During the Taliban insurgency, in January 2015, IS established itself in Khorasan and formed IS-K. The main objective of IS-K was to occupy the land of Khorasan that includes the country of Afghanistan. Even though the initial IS-K was formed by Taliban as well as Tehrik-i-Taliban Pakistan (TTP) defectors and thus ideologically similar, it became dominated by Salafists. The disgruntled members of TTP would establish IS-KP and shifted to the Nangarhar province. After its founding Pakistani leaders who defected from TTP were killed in US drone strikes, Afghan Salafists took charge of TTP.

The emergence of IS-K provided militant Afghan Salafists with an opportunity to set up a rival force, although Salafist support for the group waned as it proved ideologically "too extreme and brutal" for most Afghan Salafis. As a result, the majority of Afghan Salafis have remained supportive of the Taliban. In March 2020, major Pashtun Ahl-i Hadith ulema convened in Peshawar under the leadership of Shaikh Abdul Aziz Nooristani and Haji Hayatullah to pledge Bay'ah (oath of loyalty) to the Taliban and publicly condemn IS-K. The scholars also requested protection from the Afghan Taliban for the Ahl-i Hadith community.

After Taliban victory in the War in Afghanistan and Restoration of the Islamic Emirate, hundreds of Ahl-i Hadith ulema would gather to announce their Bay'ah (pledge of allegiance) to the Islamic Emirate of Afghanistan. Numerous Ahl-i Hadith clerics and their representatives held gatherings across various provinces of Afghanistan to re-affirm their backing of the Taliban and officially declare their support to the Taliban crackdown on IS-K. By 2016, IS-K mostly consisted of eastern Afghans, Pakistanis, and foreign fighters from Central Asia. The latter were mainly former members of the Islamic Jihad Union and the Turkistan Islamic Party. In addition, there were a small number of Arabs. Throughout its existence, IS-K has operated in a very limited area, mainly concentrated in select provinces in eastern Afghanistan, most importantly Nangarhar and Kunar. By 2016, it had appointed shadow governors in other regions as well, but not exerted much influence outside its traditional bases. The group is known to receive support by the Islamic State's central command in form of money and combat trainers from Iraq and Syria. IS-K's combat strength has fluctuated greatly over the years, but has mostly remained in the low thousands.

On 2 February, militants affiliated with IS-K killed Abdul Ghani, a Taliban commander, in Logar province. On 26 May, Asif Nang, governor of Farah province, said the Taliban have been fighting against IS militants for the past three days in Farah province. The clash left 10 Taliban and 15 IS militants dead. In May, IS-K militants captured Maulvi Abbas, a Taliban commander who was leading a small squad of insurgent fighters in Nangarhar province. In June, IS-K militants beheaded 10 Taliban fighters who were fleeing an Afghan military offensive according to a spokesman of Afghan army corps responsible for the region.

On 9 November 2015, fighting had broken out between different Taliban factions in the Zabul Province of Afghanistan. Fighters loyal to the new Taliban leader Akhtar Mansour began to fight a pro-IS faction, led by Mullah Mansoor Dadullah. According to Afghan security and local officials, Akhtar Mansour had sent as many as 450 Taliban fighters to crush Mullah Mansoor and Islamic State elements in Zabul. Dadullah's faction received support from IS during the clashes, and IS fighters also joined in on the fighting alongside Dadullah, including foreign fighters from Chechnya and Uzbekistan. Dadullah and IS were eventually defeated by Mansour's forces. Hajji Momand Nasratyar, the district governor of Arghandab, said the fighting took place in three districts of Zabul province and 86 IS militants and 26 Taliban fighters were killed in the clash. Taliban also reported to have killed several IS militants who were responsible for beheading of seven Hazara civilians a few days back.

Hajji Atta Jan, the Zabul provincial council chief, said the offensive by Mullah Mansour's fighters was so intense, that at least three Islamic State commanders, all of them ethnic Uzbeks, had surrendered. They were also asking others IS militants to do the same.[13] Radio Free Europe/Radio Liberty, while quoting sources from Southern Afghanistan, reported that some 70 IS militants were also captured in the clash by the Taliban. On 13 November, Ghulam Jelani Farahi, an Afghan police chief, said that Mullah Mansoor Dadullah was killed in a clash with Taliban.

In January 2016, hundreds of Taliban fighters launched an assault against IS bases in eastern Afghanistan. Taliban fighters were successful in capturing two districts from IS in eastern Afghanistan, but it failed to drive the group out of their stronghold in the Nazyan district in Nangarhar province. Ataullah Khogyani, a spokesman for the provincial governor, said that 26 IS militants and 5 Taliban fighters were killed in the clashes in Nangarhar. On 2 February, US carried out airstrikes targeting IS radio station in eastern Afghanistan. The strike destroyed the radio station and killed 29 IS militants. In March, Taliban factions led by Muhammad Rasul and opposed to Mansoor, began to fight against his loyalists in the group. During the fighting, dozens were reported killed. On 26 April, Hazrat Hussain Mashriqwal, a provincial police spokesman, said that 10 IS militants, including an IS commander, and 6 Taliban fighters were killed in a clash in Nangarhar. 15 IS militants and 4 Taliban fighters were also wounded during the same clash according to the spokesman.

On 19 May, local government officials reported that a clash took place between IS and Taliban in Achin and Khogyani district of Nangarhar province. 15 IS militants and 3 Taliban fighters were killed in Achin district, and the remaining were killed in Khogyani. 4 Taliban commanders were also among the dead. On 13 August, US defence officials said that ISIL's top leader, Hafiz Saeed Khan, was killed in a drone strike on 26 July in Nangarhar province. On 30 October, Ajmal Zahid, a governor of Golestan district, said that ISIL's commander, Abdul Razaq Mehdi, was killed by Taliban fighters in Farah province.

On 13 April 2017, the United States dropped the largest non-nuclear bomb, known as the GBU-43/B Massive Ordnance Air Blast (MOAB) Mother of All Bombs near Momand village upon a Nangahar's Achin District village in eastern Afghanistan to destroy tunnel complexes used by the Islamic State of Iraq and the Levant – Khorasan Province (ISIL-KP or ISIS-K).[81][82][83] The Guardian reported that following the strike, US and Afghan forces conducted clearing operations and airstrikes in the area and assessed the damage.

On 26 April, a fight occurred after IS captured 3 drug dealers who were involved in selling opium for the Taliban in Jowzjan Province. An Afghan National Police spokesman stated that the Taliban attacked IS in response, saying "The clashes erupted when group of armed Taliban attacked Daesh militants [to secure] the release of 3 drug smugglers who came here to pay 10 million afghanis [$14,780] to the Taliban for a deal." The Taliban's spokesman, Zabihullah Mujahid had also confirmed clashes were ongoing with IS at the time, without providing details on the nature of the fight or reasons. Mohammad Reza Ghafori, a spokesman for the provincial governor, said that the clashes between Taliban and IS-K had left 76 Taliban and 15 IS militants dead. IS militants also seized 2 districts from the Taliban, according to the spokesman.

On 24 May, a clash between the Taliban and IS occurred, and at that time, it had reportedly been the largest clash between the two with 22 casualties, 13 of which were IS fighters, and 9 Taliban fighters, according to a Taliban official. The clashes occurred near Iran's border with Afghanistan. The Taliban had attacked an IS camp in the area, an IS commander, who was formerly a Taliban member, said that there was an agreement between the Taliban and IS not to attack each other until there was a dialogue. The commander claimed that the Taliban had violated the agreement and attacked the IS camp. The IS commander also claimed the attack was coordinated with the Iranian military, and that there were Iranians filming dead IS fighters. The Taliban splinter faction Fidai Mahaz has also criticized the Taliban for its relationship with Iran. Days before the battle, the Taliban reportedly met with Iranian officials to discuss regional issues. A spokesman for Fidai Mahaz claimed the meeting was held at the request of the Taliban, as it was weary of the expansion of IS in the country, which also concerned the Iranian government. The spokesman also said that the Taliban received US$3 million in cash, 3,000 arms, 40 trucks, and the ammunition from Iran's intelligence services, in order to fight IS near the Iranian border, although a Taliban spokesman denied the allegations.

On 27 November, Taliban executed one of its senior commanders for colluding with IS. A week before, IS fighters were mass executed by their fellow militants in Achin district, according to a provincial government spokesman. However, the spokesman did not provide any additional detail, and neither did IS release any official statement on killing its own members.

On 20 June 2018, after the talks between the Russian government and the Taliban, US assistant secretary of state Alice Wells condemned the Russian government's position on the Taliban that included backing for the group against IS, stating it gave the Taliban legitimacy and challenged the recognized Afghan government. In July, the Taliban launched an offensive against IS in the Jowzjan province. According to a surrendered IS commander, the Taliban had amassed 2,000 fighters for the offensive against IS. The fighters from the Islamic Movement of Uzbekistan, who had sworn allegiance to IS, were also present fighting alongside IS against the Taliban. During the fighting, 3,500 to 7,000 civilians were displaced. By the end of July, IS's hold in the region was reduced to 2 villages, all thanks to the Taliban's campaign. In response, they requested support from the Afghan government, and also agreed to put down their arms in exchange for protection from the Taliban.

The Afghan Air Force later carried out airstrikes against the Taliban in exchange for IS's surrender in the region. The agreement between the Afghan government and IS created controversy afterwards. On 17 July, IS militants killed 15 Taliban militants and injured 5 others during a raid on a house belonging to a Taliban commander in Sar-e Pol. Abdul Qayuom Baqizoi, the police chief of Sar-e Pol, told Associated Press that Taliban and IS fighters have been fighting each other in Jowzjan and Sar-e Pol for more than two months, killing hundreds on both sides.

In August, during the negotiations between the US government and the Taliban in Doha, the Taliban had requested that the US ends airstrikes on the Taliban, as well as provide support to the group in order to fight IS. On 22 June 2019, clashes were reported in Kunar between the Taliban and IS, by an Afghan government official. The official also claimed that the Afghan military had killed some IS fighters in the area, and that the Taliban was active in the area as well.

In March 2020, the Afghan Salafist Council under its emir, Shaikh Abdul Aziz Nooristani, met with Taliban leaders and plegded loyalty to their movement. Salafists had previously provided crucial support to IS-K, but recognized that the latter's position had greatly declined after its defeats in Nangarhar and Kunar. The Salafist Council, represented by 32 scholars and military leaders, stated that they were in no way loyal to IS-K, and wanted to be left out of the Islamic State–Taliban conflict. The Taliban leadership accepted the pledge of loyalty, exploiting it in its propaganda.

In October 2020, former Politico reporter Wesley Morgan revealed that United States special operations forces, longtime foes of the Taliban, had been conducting drone strikes against IS-K to give the Taliban an advantage in the field. According to Morgan, the operators were jokingly referred to as the "Taliban Air Force" and instead of communicating directly with Taliban commanders, they would monitor Taliban communications and decide when the best time was to strike. On 10 December 2020, General Kenneth McKenzie Jr., head of U.S. Central Command, confirmed that the U.S. had assisted the Taliban via opportunistic drone strikes, saying that they did not coordinate operations with the Taliban, but took advantage of them fighting a "common enemy" to conduct their own operations. Gen. McKenzie said the strikes occurred several months prior when IS-K was holding ground in Nangarhar Province and elsewhere in eastern Afghanistan.

The Taliban finally succeeded in taking over Afghanistan from the Islamic Republic during a large-scale offensive in summer 2021. Kabul fell on 15 August 2021, prompting the leaders of the IS-K to denounce the Taliban takeover of Afghanistan. The Taliban immediately moved to contain or purge potential opponents, including Islamic State supporters and Salafists. Across the country, the Taliban ordered the closure of Salafist mosques seminaries and tried to arrest prominent Salafist scholars, prompting many to go into hiding. Among those targeted by the new Taliban authorities were Salafi clerics who had publicly opposed IS-K.

Researcher Abdul Sayed argued that the purge was probably organized by hardline anti-Salafist elements within the Taliban and more motivated by long-time resentment than fears about Salafi support for a future IS-K insurgency. On 16 August, the Taliban claimed to have killed around 150 IS-K fighters, including its former chief Abu Umar Khurasani, while prisoners were being released from a jail in Kabul. However, many IS-K militants were able to rejoin the IS-K ranks because of spree of prison breaks across the country organized by the Taliban. On 26 August, a suicide bombing and a mass shooting occurred near Abbey Gate at Hamid Karzai International Airport in Kabul, Afghanistan. The attack began hours after the United States' State Department told Americans outside the airport to leave due to a terrorist threat. At least 185 people were killed in the attacks, including 13 U.S. service members. The Taliban condemned the attack, saying "evil circles will be strictly stopped". The Taliban later announced that they would take every possible measure to capture IS-KP leader Shahab al-Muhajir. The same day, Saifullah Mohammed, Taliban's CID chief, told The Times that they had captured 6 militants belonging to IS-K following a gun battle in western side of Kabul.

Taliban militants kidnapped the influential Salafi cleric, Mullah Abu Obaidullah Mutawakil on 28 August; he was "brutal" murdered one week later. Taliban spokesman Zabiullah Mujahid denied the Taliban's role in the killing of Mutawakil, but also did not condemn the murder. Even though Mutawakil was described as an IS-K sympathiser and a large number of his students were part of IS-K, he had not officially backed the Islamic State. IS-K did not offer prayers for him after his demise, stating that he had not been loyal to the Islamic State's caliphate. On 9 November 2021, Reuters journalist James MacKenzie stated that "frequent, smaller atrocities" in the conflict are "less commonly reported." Aside from the ISIS stronghold of Nangarhar, other affected areas include Ghazni in central Afghanistan, Herat in the west, Balkh in the north, and Paktia, Paktika and Khost in the southeast.

On 24 October 2021, a bomb attack in Afghanistan has left at least 2 civilians dead on Saturday, 1 being a child, and four wounded. The device placed on the road in eastern Afghanistan was aimed at a Taliban vehicle.[146] On the same day, it was reported that ISKP had raised a flag in a village in Uruzgan Province and that the militants were distributing leaflets at mosques in nearby villages. On 25 October, 17 people were killed in clashes between gunmen and Taliban forces in Herat. On the same day it was announced that Tajikistan and China had reached an agreement for China to fund construction for a new Tajik military base and that Chinese forces can completely operate a military base near the Afghan border.

On 31 October, at least a hundred IS militants reportedly surrendered to the Taliban security forces in Nangarhar province, as part of an operation to suppress the insurgent formation in the country. In the month of October, a former Afghan national army officer, who recently joined ISKP ranks, was killed in clash with Taliban fighters. The former officer commanded the Afghan military's weapons and ammunition depot in Gardez before the Taliban takeover.

Since the Taliban takeover, the violence in Nangahar province has escalated with near-daily attacks claimed by the Islamic State. The Taliban responded by deploying an additional 1,300 fighters in the province in the month of October with the aim to increase the number of operations conducted against the ISKP fighters in the province. Talibans have also carried out night raids against suspected ISKP fighters in the province and many of the hundreds arrested during those raids have either disappeared or turned up dead. The Taliban's harsh crackdown in the province against the suspected ISKP fighters has resulted in a number of human right violations by the Taliban fighters, according to Nangahar residents. Islamic State has also used Taliban's harsh crackdown as a part of its recruitment propaganda calling on Nangahar residents to rise up and resist the Taliban. Nangahar residents say that the Taliban fighters in the province are not familiar with the area and have no way to check the intelligence they receive about Islamic State targets. So the Taliban fighters have started killing anyone they suspect of working for the Islamic State, according to the residents. Washington Post reports that only a few Taliban fighters have the necessary training or experience to conduct precision-based operations in urban areas. As the Taliban are more adopted to guerrilla warfare, they are therefore still adjusting to maintain security during peacetime.

By early November, IS-KP in Nangahar was repeatedly assassinating ex-republicans and pro-Taliban figures and attacked patrols with such a frequency that the Taliban government ordered its fighters in the province to no longer leave settlements at night. On 2 November, the 2021 Kabul hospital attack took place where assailants attacked the Daoud Khan Military Hospital with guns and suicide bombers killing at least 25 people and wounding at least 50 more people. A senior Taliban commander, Mawlawi Hamdullah Mukhlis, was killed in the attack. He was the head of the Kabul military corps and was 1 of the first "senior" Taliban commanders to enter the abandoned Afghan presidential palace on August 15. The Taliban blamed ISKP for the attack and claimed that they killed at least 4 militants in a shootout. On the same day, ISIL claimed responsibility for killing a Taliban judge in a gun attack in PD-2, Jalalabad.

On 11 April 2022 Islamic State transforms and grows in Pakistan and Afghanistan according to a report by the AP news agency- A concerted focus on "social media warfare" is critical to advance on the ideological battlefield but also in order to counter the pull of "enchanting" social media influencers, ISIS Khorasan declared in a new issue of the group's English-language magazine. In their magazine "Voice of Khurasan", ISIS Khorasan criticized the management and thinking of the Taliban. On April 19, 2022, At least 6 people have been killed and 17 injured in bomb attacks on two schools in Kabul. The students who attended these centers are from the Shiite Hazara minority, which is the population that lives in the Dashte Barchi neighborhood to the west of the Afghan capital. The Taliban spokesman for the Ministry of the Interior has warned that the death toll could increase. Several injured are in serious condition. No one has immediately claimed responsibility for the attacks but it is suspected that the Afghan affiliate of the Islamic State is guilty of the events.

The Afghan affiliate of the Islamic State extremist group has claimed responsibility for a series of attacks against the country's Shiite minority during the week of April 18–24, 2022. The bomb attack on a mosque and religious school in northern Afghanistan, from April 22, caused the death of 33 people, including students. Added to these attacks are those that occurred in two educational centers in the Shiite Hazara minority neighborhood of Dashte Barchi, in western Kabul, causing at least six deaths and 25 injuries, according to official data. Several smaller explosions in recent days in different parts of Afghanistan, including another detonation today in a Kabul neighborhood that initially caused no casualties. There was also a roadside mine explosion yesterday in the eastern province of Nangarhar, which left at least four members of the Taliban security forces dead and one wounded. In the city of Kunduz, another detonation against a vehicle left four dead and 18 injured, including children. The Taliban announced the arrest of a former leader of IS-K in the northern region of Balkh, whose capital is Mazar-e-Sharif.

On Friday, April 29, 2022, the last day of the holy month of Ramadan, there was a new attack against a Sufi Mosque in Afghanistan as part of the wave of violence that is sweeping the country. The explosion occurred in the west of the capital, Kabul, during prayers and killed 50 people. The same day two high-voltage towers in Parwan province were bombed on the night of Friday, April 29, 2022, cutting off electricity to the capital and neighboring provinces.

Chapter 9
Grand Mosque seizure

The Grand Mosque seizure in Mecca occurred during November and December 1979 when extremist insurgents calling for the overthrow of the House of Saud took over Masjid al-Haram, the holiest mosque in Islam, in Mecca, Saudi Arabia. The insurgents declared that the Mahdi (the "redeemer of Islam") had arrived in the form of one of their leaders – Mohammed Abdullah al-Qahtani – and called on Muslims to obey him. The Saudi Arabian Army, advised by French GIGN forces, fought for almost two weeks to reclaim the Grand Mosque.

The seizure of Islam's holiest site, the taking of hostages from among the worshippers and the deaths of hundreds of militants, security forces and hostages caught in the crossfire in the ensuing battles for control of the site, shocked the Islamic world. The siege ended two weeks after the takeover began, with the mosque being cleared.[9] Al-Qahtani was killed in the recapture of the mosque, but leader Juhayman al-Otaybi and 67 of his fellow rebels who survived the assault were captured and later beheaded. Following the attack, the Saudi King Khaled implemented a stricter enforcement of Shariah (Islamic law) and he gave the ulama and religious conservatives more power over the next decade, and the religious police became more assertive.

The seizure was led by Juhayman al-Otaybi, a member of the Otaibah family, influential in Najd. He declared his brother-in-law Mohammed Abdullah al-Qahtani to be the Mahdi, or redeemer, who is believed to arrive on earth several years before Judgment Day. His followers embellished the fact that Al-Qahtani's name and his father's name are identical to the Prophet Mohammed's name and that of his father, and developed a saying, "His and his father's names were the same as Mohammed's and his father's, and he had come to Makkah from the north," to justify their belief. The date of the attack, 20 November 1979, was the first day of the year 1400 according to the Islamic calendar; this ties in with the tradition of the mujaddid, a person who appears at the turn of every century of the Islamic calendar to revive Islam, cleansing it of extraneous elements and restoring it to its pristine purity.

Juhayman's grandfather, Sultan bin Bajad al-Otaybi, had ridden with Ibn Saud in the early decades of the century, and other Otaibah family members were among foremost of the Ikhwan. Juhayman acted as a preacher, a corporal in the Saudi National Guard, and was a former student of Sheikh Abd al-Aziz Ibn Baz, who went on to become the Grand Mufti of Saudi Arabia. Al-Otaybi had turned against Ibn Baz "and began advocating a return to the original ways of Islam, among other things: a repudiation of the West; abolition of television and expulsion of non-Muslims." He proclaimed that "the ruling Al-Saud dynasty had lost its legitimacy because it was corrupt, ostentatious and had destroyed Saudi culture by an aggressive policy of Westernization."

Al-Otaybi and Qahtani had met while imprisoned together for sedition, when al-Otaybi claimed to have had a vision sent by God telling him that Qahtani was the Mahdi. Their declared goal was to institute a theocracy in preparation for the imminent apocalypse. They differed from the original Ikhwan and other earlier Wahhabi purists in that "they were millenarians, they rejected the monarchy and condemned the Wahhabi ulama." Many of their followers were drawn from theology students at the Islamic University in Medina. Al-Otaybi joined the local chapter of the Salafi group Al-Jamaa Al-Salafiya Al-Muhtasiba (The Salafi Group That Commands Right and Forbids Wrong) in Medina headed by Sheikh Abd al-Aziz Ibn Baz, chairman of the Permanent Committee for Islamic Research and Issuing Fatwas at the time.

The followers preached their radical message in different mosques in Saudi Arabia without being arrested, and the government was reluctant to confront religious extremists. When Al-Otaybi, al-Qahtani and a number of the Ikhwan were locked up as troublemakers by the Ministry of Interior security police, the Mabahith, in 1978. Members of the ulama (including Ibn Baz) cross-examined them for heresy but they were subsequently released as being traditionalists harkening back to the Ikhwan, like al-Otaybi's grandfather and, therefore, not a threat.

Even after the seizure of the Grand Mosque, a certain level of forbearance by ulama for the rebels remained. When the government asked for a fatwa allowing armed force in the Grand Mosque, the language of Ibn Baz and other senior ulama "was curiously restrained." The scholars did not declare al-Otaybi and his followers non-Muslims, despite their violation of the sanctity of the Grand Mosque, but only termed them "al-jamaah al-musallahah" (the armed group). The senior scholars also insisted that before security forces attack them, the authorities must offer them the option to surrender.

Because of donations from wealthy followers, the group was well-armed and trained. Some members, like al-Otaybi, were former military officials of the National Guard. Some National Guard troops sympathetic to the insurgents smuggled weapons, ammunition, gas masks and provisions into the mosque compound over a period of weeks before the New Year. Automatic weapons were smuggled from National Guard armories and the supplies were hidden in the hundreds of small underground rooms under the mosque that were used as hermitages.

In the early morning of 20 November 1979, the imam of the Grand Mosque, Sheikh Mohammed al-Subayil, was preparing to lead prayers for the 50,000 worshippers who had gathered for prayer. At around 5:00 am he was interrupted by insurgents who produced weapons from under their robes, chained the gates shut and killed two policemen who were armed with only wooden clubs for disciplining unruly pilgrims. The number of insurgents has been given as "at least 500" or "four to five hundred", and included several women and children who had joined al-Otaybi's movement.

At the time the Grand Mosque was being renovated by the Saudi Binladin Group. An employee of the organization was able to report the seizure to the outside world before the insurgents cut the telephone lines. The insurgents released most of the hostages and locked the remainder in the sanctuary. They took defensive positions in the upper levels of the mosque, and sniper positions in the minarets, from which they commanded the grounds. No one outside the mosque knew how many hostages remained, how many militants were in the mosque and what sort of preparations they had made.

At the time of the event, Crown Prince Fahd was in Tunisia for a meeting of the Arab League Summit. The commander of the National Guard, Prince Abdullah, was also abroad for an official visit to Morocco. Therefore, King Khalid assigned the responsibility to two members of the Sudairi Seven – Prince Sultan, then Minister of Defence, and Prince Nayef, then Minister of Interior, to deal with the incident. Soon after the rebel seizure, about 100 security officers of the Ministry of Interior attempted to retake the mosque, but were turned back with heavy casualties. The survivors were quickly joined by units of the Saudi Arabian Army and Saudi Arabian National Guard. At the request of the Saudi monarchy, French GIGN units, operatives and commandos were rushed to assist Saudi forces in Mecca. By evening the entire city of Mecca had been evacuated. Prince Sultan appointed Turki bin Faisal Al Saud, head of the Al Mukhabaraat Al 'Aammah (Saudi Intelligence), to take over the forward command post several hundred meters from the mosque, where Prince Turki would remain for the next several weeks. However, the first task was to seek the approval of the ulama, which was led by Abdul Aziz Ibn Baz. Islam forbids any violence within the Grand Mosque, to the extent that plants cannot be uprooted without explicit religious sanction. Ibn Baz found himself in a delicate situation, especially as he had previously taught al-Otaybi in Medina. Regardless, the ulema issued a fatwa allowing deadly force to be used in retaking the mosque.

With religious approval granted, Saudi forces launched frontal assaults on three of the main gates. Again, the assaulting forces were repulsed. Snipers continued to pick off soldiers who revealed themselves. The insurgents aired their demands from the mosque's loudspeakers throughout the streets of Mecca, calling for the cut-off of oil exports to the United States and the expulsion of all foreign civilian and military experts from the Arabian Peninsula. In Beirut, an opposition organization, the Arab Socialist Action Party – Arabian Peninsula, issued a statement on 25 November, alleging to clarify the demands of the insurgents. The party, however, denied any involvement in the seizure of the Grand Mosque.

Officially, the Saudi government took the position that it would not aggressively retake the mosque, but rather starve out the militants. Nevertheless, several unsuccessful assaults were undertaken, at least one of them through the underground tunnels in and around the mosque. A team of three French commandos from the Groupe d'Intervention de la Gendarmerie Nationale (GIGN) arrived in Mecca. The commandos pumped gas into the underground chambers, but perhaps because the rooms were so bafflingly interconnected, the gas failed and the resistance continued. With casualties climbing, Saudi forces drilled holes into the courtyard and dropped grenades into the rooms below, indiscriminately killing many hostages but driving the remaining rebels into more open areas where they could be picked off by sharpshooters. More than two weeks after the assault began, the surviving rebels finally surrendered.

However, this account is contradicted by at least two other accounts,[38][page needed] including that of then GIGN commanding officer Christian Prouteau: the three GIGN commandos trained and equipped the Saudi forces and devised their attack plan (which consisted of drilling holes in the floor of the Mosque and firing gas canisters wired with explosives through the perforations), but did not take part in the action and did not set foot in the Mosque. The Saudi National Guard and the Saudi Army suffered heavy casualties. Tear gas was used to force out the remaining militants. According to a US embassy cable made on 1 December, several of the militant leaders escaped the siege and days later sporadic fighting erupted in other parts of the city. The battle had lasted for more than two weeks, and had officially left "255 pilgrims, troops and fanatics" killed and "another 560 injured, although diplomats suggested the toll was higher." Military casualties were 127 dead and 451 injured.

Chapter 10
Jerusalem Crisis

Jerusalem is the holy place of all the three Abrahmic religions – Judaism, Christianity and Islam. But see how they have made it a hell. A major outbreak of violence in the ongoing Israeli–Palestinian conflict commenced on 10 May 2021, though disturbances took place earlier, and continued until a ceasefire came into effect on 21 May. It was marked by protests and police riot control, rocket attacks on Israel by Hamas and Palestinian Islamic Jihad (PIJ), and Israeli airstrikes in the Gaza Strip. The crisis was triggered on 6 May, when Palestinians in East Jerusalem began protesting over an anticipated decision of the Supreme Court of Israel on the eviction of six Palestinian families in the neighborhood of Sheikh Jarrah. Under international law, the area, effectively annexed by Israel in 1980, is a part of the Palestinian Territories; Israel applies its laws there. On 7 May, according to Israel's Channel 12, Palestinians threw stones at Israeli police forces, who then stormed the Al-Aqsa Mosque compound using tear gas, rubber bullets, and stun grenades. The crisis prompted protests around the world as well as official reactions from world leaders.

The violence coincided with Qadr Night (8 May), observed by Muslims, and Jerusalem Day (9–10 May), an Israeli national holiday. The confrontations occurred ahead of a planned Jerusalem Day parade known as the Dance of Flags by far-right Jewish nationalists, which was later canceled. More than 600 people were injured, mostly Palestinians, drawing international condemnation. Israel's Supreme Court ruling on evictions from Sheikh Jarrah was then delayed for 30 days as Avichai Mandelblit, the erstwhile attorney general of Israel, sought to reduce tensions.

On the afternoon of 10 May, Hamas gave Israel an ultimatum to withdraw its security forces from both the Temple Mount complex and Sheikh Jarrah by 6 p.m. When the ultimatum expired without a response, both Hamas and PIJ launched rockets from the Gaza Strip into Israel; some of these rockets hit Israeli residences and a school. Israel then began a campaign of airstrikes against Gaza; by 16 May, some 950 targeted attacks had demolished, completely or partially: 18 buildings, including four high-rise towers; 40 schools and four hospitals; and also struck the al-Shati refugee camp. Additionally, at least 19 medical facilities were damaged or destroyed by the Israeli bombardment. By 17 May, the United Nations estimated that Israeli airstrikes had destroyed 94 buildings in Gaza, comprising 461 housing and commercial units, including the al-Jalaa Highrise; housing offices of the Associated Press, the Al Jazeera Media Network, and other news outlets; and 60 condominiums.

As a result of the violence, at least 256 Palestinians, including 66 children, were killed (including at least seven from friendly fire). In Israel, at least 13 people were killed, including two children. The Gaza Ministry of Health reported that more than 1,900 Palestinians were injured, and as of 12 May, at least 200 Israelis were reported to have been injured. As of 19 May, at least 72,000 Palestinians have been displaced. Around 4,360 Palestinian rockets were fired towards Israel, of which 680 landed within the Gaza Strip, and over 90 percent of rockets bound towards populated areas were intercepted by Israel's Iron Dome. Israel conducted around 1,500 aerial, land, and sea strikes on the Gaza Strip.

Calls for a ceasefire were first proposed on 13 May by Hamas, but rejected by Israeli Prime Minister Benjamin Netanyahu. On 18 May, France, along with Egypt and Jordan, announced the filing of a United Nations Security Council resolution for a ceasefire. Egypt mediated a ceasefire between Israel and Hamas, which came into effect on 21 May 2021, ending 11 days of fighting in which both sides claimed victory. On 16 June 2021, incendiary balloons were launched from Gaza into Israel, which the Israeli Air Force responded to with multiple airstrikes in the Gaza Strip, resuming the fighting.

At the beginning of the Muslim holy month of Ramadan in 2021, Jerusalem Islamic Waqf officials said that on the night of 13 April, the Israeli police entered the Al-Aqsa Mosque compound and severed the loudspeaker cables used to broadcast the muezzin's ritual call to prayer so that the Memorial Day speech being delivered by President Reuven Rivlin below at the Western Wall would not be disturbed. Israeli police declined to comment. The incident was condemned by Jordan, and the Palestinian National Authority President Mahmoud Abbas called the incident "a racist hate crime", but it did not draw other international attention.

Same month Israeli police closed the staired plaza outside the Old City's Damascus Gate, a traditional holiday gathering spot for Palestinians. The closure triggered violent night clashes, the barricades were removed after several days. On 15 April, a TikTok video of a Palestinian teen slapping an ultra-orthodox Jewish man went viral, leading to several copycat incidents. The next day, tens of thousands of Palestinian worshippers were turned away from al-Aqsa, on the first Friday of Ramadan when Israel imposed a 10,000-person limit on prayers at the mosque. On the same day, a rabbi was beaten in Jaffa causing two days of protests. On 22 April, the far-right Jewish supremacist group Lehava held a march through Jerusalem chanting "death to Arabs." On 23 April, after fringe military groups fired 36 rockets at southern Israel, the IDF launched missiles at Hamas targets in the Gaza Strip.

The barrage of rocket fire came as hundreds of Palestinians clashed with Israeli police in East Jerusalem and on 25 April, the United Nations envoy Tor Wennesland condemned the violence and said, "The provocative acts across Jerusalem must cease. The indiscriminate launching of rockets towards Israeli population centers violates international law and must stop immediately." On 26 April, after more than 40 rockets have been launched from the Gaza Strip into Israel while one projectile exploded inside the Gaza Strip over of the previous three days, the Security Cabinet of Israel voted in favor after an hours-long debate of an operational plan to strike Hamas if rocket fire from Gaza continues. In the following days, a Palestinian boy and a 19-year-old Israeli settler were killed. On 6 May, the Israel Police shot and killed a 16-year-old Palestinian during a raid of Nablus in the West Bank. According to Addameer, Israeli police arrested at least 61 children from mid-April during clashes in and about East Jerusalem, and 4 were shot dead in three weeks.

The Sheikh Jarrah district houses the descendants of refugees expelled or displaced from their homes in Jaffa and Haifa in the Nakba of 1948. Today, around 75 Palestinian families live on this disputed land. The long-running dispute over land ownership in Sheikh Jarrah is considered a microcosm of the Israeli–Palestinian disputes over land since 1948. Currently, more than 1,000 Palestinians living across East Jerusalem face possible eviction. Israeli law allows Israeli land owners to file claims over land in East Jerusalem which they have owned prior to 1948, except where expropriated by the Jordanian government, but rejects Palestinian claims over land in Israel which they owned.[86] The international community considers East Jerusalem to be Palestinian territory held under Israeli occupation and the Office of the United Nations High Commissioner for Human Rights (OHCHR) has called on Israel to stop all forced evictions of Palestinians from Sheikh Jarrah, saying that if carried out the expulsions of the Palestinians would violate Israel's responsibilities under international law which prohibit the transfer of civilians in to or out of occupied territory by the occupying power.

A spokesman for the OHCHR said that such transfers may constitute a "war crime". Human rights organizations have been critical of Israeli efforts to remove Palestinians from Sheikh Jarrah, with Human Rights Watch releasing a statement saying that the disparate rights between Palestinian and Jewish residents of East Jerusalem "underscores the reality of apartheid that Palestinians in East Jerusalem face." Israeli human rights group estimate that over 1,000 Palestinian families are at risk of eviction in East Jerusalem.

A Jewish trust bought the land in Sheikh Jarrah from Arab landowners in the 1870s in Ottoman Palestine. However, the purchase is disputed by some Palestinians, who have produced Ottoman-era land titles for part of the land. The land came under Jordanian control following the 1948 Arab–Israeli War. Following the war, Jewish residents were expelled from East Jerusalem, and Palestinians from Israel. In 1956, the

Jordanian government, in cooperation with the United Nations' organization for refugees, housed 28 of these Palestinian families on land owned by Jewish trusts.[83][90] After the Six-Day War the area fell under Israeli occupation. In 1970, Israel passed a law that allowed previous owners to reclaim property in East Jerusalem that had been taken by Jordan without having ownership transferred. Under this law, in 1972, the Israeli Custodian General registered the properties under the Jewish trusts which claimed to be the rightful owners of the land

In 1982, an agreement was endorsed by the courts which the families later said had been made without their knowledge and disputed the original ownership claims by the Jewish trusts. These challenges were rejected by Israeli courts. The trusts then demanded that the tenants pay rent. Eviction orders began to be issued in the 1990s. Palestinian tenants say that Israeli courts have no jurisdiction in the area since the land is outside Israel's recognized borders; this view is supported by the UN Human Rights Office.

In 2003, the Jewish trusts sold the homes to a right-wing settler organization, which then made repeated attempts to evict the Palestinian residents. The company has submitted plans to build more than 200 housing units, which have not yet[when?] been approved by the government.[83] These groups succeeded in evicting 43 Palestinians from the area in 2002, and three more families since then. In 2010, the Supreme Court of Israel rejected an appeal by Palestinian families who had resided in 57 housing units in the area of Sheikh Jarrah, who had petitioned the court to have their ownership to the properties recognized. An Israeli court had previously ruled that the Palestinians could remain on the properties under a legal status called "protected tenants", but had to pay rent. The move to evict them came after they refused to pay rent and carried out construction.

In 2021 Israel's Supreme Court was expected to deliver a ruling on whether to uphold the eviction of six Palestinian families from the Sheikh Jarrah neighborhood on 10 May 2021, after a court ruled that 13 families comprising 58 people had to vacate the properties by 1 August. On 9 May 2021, the Israeli Supreme Court delayed the expected decision on evictions for 30 days, after an intervention from Attorney General of Israel Avichai Mandelblit. On 26 May 2021, the court ordered Mandelblit to submit his legal opinion on the matter within two weeks. In a related case, the Jerusalem District Court is holding a hearing on appeals filed on behalf of seven families subject of eviction orders from the Batan al-Hawa section of Silwan. According to Haaretz, Mandelblit notified the court on 7 June that he would decline to present a view on the case; a new hearing date of 2 August was set.

According to the Jerusalem Institute for Policy Research, this approach to property rights is unacceptable in international law. The Jerusalem-based non-profit organization B'Tselem and the international Human Rights Watch cited discriminatory policies in East Jerusalem in recent reports, alleging that Israel is guilty of the crime of apartheid. Israel rejected the allegations. East Jerusalem is effectively annexed by Israel, and Israel applies its laws there. According to the Office of the United Nations High Commissioner for Human Rights, the area is a part of the Palestinian territories that Israel currently occupies. United States Secretary of State Antony Blinken warned Israel that evicting Palestinian families from their homes in East Jerusalem is among the actions by both sides that could lead to "conflict and war."

The 2021 Palestinian legislative election for the Palestinian Legislative Council, originally scheduled for 22 May 2021, was indefinitely postponed on 29 April by President Mahmoud Abbas. Hamas, which was expected to do well in the elections, called the move a "coup", and some Palestinians believed Abbas had delayed the election to avoid political defeat for his party Fatah. Analysts say the postponement contributed towards the current crisis, and encouraged Hamas to resort to military confrontation rather than diplomatic tactics. Opinion pieces in NBC News, the Wall Street Journal and Foreign Policy argued that by taking responsibility for the rocket fire, Hamas had improved its standing among Palestinians wary of the delayed elections. In Israel, the 2019–2021 Israeli political crisis saw four inconclusive elections which left Israel functioning under a caretaker government. Prime Minister Benjamin Netanyahu was trying to persuade several extreme-right politicians to form a coalition. The presence of right-wing Israeli politicians Ben-Gvir and King contributed to the crisis. The New York Times said Netanyahu was trying to instigate a crisis to build support for his leadership, and thus allowed tensions to rise in Jerusalem. An article in The Conversation dismissed this as "conspiratorial", arguing that although the crisis has given Netanyahu a political opportunity, he "was not looking or hoping for a major conflict with the Palestinians to help him hold onto power".

Al-Aqsa Mosque compound

On 7 May, large numbers of police were deployed on the Temple Mount as around 70,000 worshippers attended the final Friday prayers of Ramadan at al-Aqsa. After the evening prayers, some Palestinian worshippers began throwing previously stockpiled rocks and other objects at Israeli police officers. Police officers fired stun grenades into the mosque compound, and into a field clinic. A mosque spokesman stated the clashes broke out after Israeli police attempted to evacuate the compound, where many Palestinians sleep over in Ramadan, adding that the evacuation was intended to allow access to Israelis. More than 300 Palestinians were wounded as Israeli police stormed the mosque compound. Palestinians threw rocks, firecrackers, and heavy objects, while Israeli police fired stun grenades, tear gas, and rubber bullets at worshippers. The storming came ahead of a Jerusalem Day flag march by Jewish nationalists through the Old City. More than 600 Palestinians were injured, more than 400 of whom were hospitalized. Militants in Gaza fired rockets into Israel the following night.

More clashes occurred on 8 May, the date of the Islamic holy night of Laylat al-Qadr. Palestinian crowds threw stones, lit fires, and chanted "Strike Tel Aviv" and "In spirit and in blood, we will redeem al-Aqsa", which The Times of Israel described as in support of Hamas. The Israel Police, wearing riot gear and some on horseback, used stun grenades and water cannons. At least 80 people were injured. Also on 10 May, a video showing a tree burning near al-Aqsa began to circulate on social media. Below in the Western plaza, a crowd of Jewish Israelis was singing and dancing in celebration of Jerusalem Day. Yair Wallach accused them of singing "genocidal songs of vengeance." The crowd cheered the flames with words from a song from Judges 16:28 in which Samson cries out before he tears down the pillars in Gaza, "O God, that I may with one blow take vengeance on the Philistines for my two eyes!" Witnesses differed as to whether the fire was caused by an Israeli police stun grenade or by fireworks thrown by Palestinian protesters. Although the fire happened just 10 meters away from al-Aqsa, there was no damage to the mosque.

After Friday prayers on 14 May, Palestinians protested in more than 200 locations in the West Bank. Protesters hurled stones and Israeli soldiers responded with live fire and tear gas. As a result, 11 Palestinians were killed in the clashes. A Palestinian man who attempted to stab a soldier was shot, but survived; no Israeli soldiers were wounded in the incident. More than 100 Palestinians were injured. There have been daily demonstrations since the escalation in Gaza. As of 16 May, a total of 13 Palestinians had been killed in the West Bank in clashes with Israeli troops by 14 May. On 17 May, three Palestinian demonstrators were killed in clashes with the IDF.

According to Al Arabiya, Fatah has backed a call for a general strike on 18 May in the West Bank, including East Jerusalem. Palestinians in Israel have been asked to take part. In an unusual display of unity by "Palestinian citizens of Israel, who make up 20% of its population, and those in the territories Israel seized in 1967" the strike went ahead and "shops were shuttered across cities in Gaza, the occupied West Bank and in villages and towns inside Israel". During the day of protests and strikes, a Palestinian man was killed and more than 70 wounded in clashes near Ramallah and two Israeli soldiers were injured in a shooting attack. Large crowds also gathered in Nablus, Bethlehem and Hebron while police deployed water cannons in Sheikh Jarrah.

Arab communities in Israel

During the evening and night of 10 May, Arab rioters in Lod threw stones and firebombs at Jewish homes, a school, and a synagogue, later attacking a hospital. Shots were fired at the rioters, killing one and wounding two; a Jewish suspect in the shooting was arrested. Widespread protests and riots intensified across Israel, particularly in cities with large Arab populations. In Lod, rocks were thrown at Jewish apartments and some Jewish residents were evacuated from their homes by the police. Synagogues and a Muslim cemetery were vandalized. A Jewish man was critically wounded after being struck in the head by a brick, and died six days later. In Acre, the Effendi hotel was torched by Arab rioters, injuring several guests. One of them, Avi Har-Even, a former head of the Israel Space Agency, suffered burns and smoke inhalation, and died on 6 June.

In the nearby city of Ramle, Jewish rioters threw rocks at passing vehicles. On 11 May, Mayor of Lod Yair Revivio urged Prime Minister of Israel Benjamin Netanyahu to deploy the Israel Border Police to the city, stating that the municipality had "completely lost control" and warning that the country was on the brink of "civil war". Netanyahu declared a state of emergency in Lod on 11 May, marking the first time since 1966 that Israel has used emergency powers over an Arab community. Border Police forces were deployed to the city. A nighttime curfew was declared and entry to the city was prohibited for non-resident civilians. Minister of Public Security Amir Ohana announced the implementation of emergency orders.

Unrest continued on 12 May. In Acre, a Jewish man was attacked and seriously injured by an Arab mob armed with sticks and stones while driving his car. In Bat Yam, Jewish extremists attacked Arab stores and beat pedestrians. An Arab motorist was pulled from his car and severely beaten in the street. The incident was caught live by an Israeli news crew.

As of 13 May, communal violence including "riots, stabbings, arson, attempted home invasions and shootings" was reported from Beersheba, Rahat, Ramla, Lod, Nasiriyah, Tiberias, Jerusalem, Haifa and Acre. An Israeli soldier was severely beaten in Jaffa and hospitalized for a skull fracture and cerebral hemorrhage, a Jewish paramedic and another Jewish man were shot in separate incidents in Lod, a police officer was shot in Ramla, Israeli journalists were attacked by far-right rioters in Tel Aviv, and a Jewish family that mistakenly drove into Umm al-Fahm was attacked by an Arab mob before being rescued by other local residents and police. Israel Border Police forces were deployed throughout the country to quell the unrest, and 10 Border Police reserve companies were called up. In an address to police in Lod, Prime Minister Netanyahu told them not to worry about future commissions of inquiry and investigations into their enforcement during the riots, reminding them of the way the police had suppressed the Palestinian Land Day riots of 1976.

By 17 May, the rioting had mostly died down. However, on 18 May, Israeli-Arabs, together with Palestinians in the West Bank and Gaza Strip, held a general strike in protest against Israeli policies toward Palestinians. Numerous employers threatened to fire Arab workers who participated in the strike. The management of Rambam Hospital in Haifa sent letters to their Arab employees warning against participating in the strike, and the Ministry of Education came under heavy criticism from teachers throughout Israel after it sent requests to the principals of schools in Arab towns asking for a list of teachers who participated in the strike. There were some instances of employees who participated in the strike being unlawfully dismissed without a prior hearing as required under Israeli law. The Israeli telecommunications company Cellcom paused work for an hour as an act in support of coexistence. The move led to calls for a boycott of Cellcom among Israeli right-wingers who accused it of showing solidarity with the strike, and several Jewish settlement councils and right-wing organizations cut ties with it. Cellcom's stock subsequently dropped by two percent.

Throughout the riots, Arab rioters set 10 synagogues and 112 Jewish homes on fire, looted 386 Jewish homes and damaged another 673, and set 849 Jewish cars on fire. There were also 5,018 recorded instances of stone-throwing against Jews. By contrast, Jewish rioters damaged 13 Arab homes and set 13 Arab cars on fire, and there were 41 recorded instances of stone-throwing against Arabs. One Arab home was set on fire by Arab rioters who mistook it for a Jewish home. No mosques were set on fire and no Arab homes were reported looted during the unrest. By 19 May, 1,319 people had been arrested for participating in the riots, of whom 159 were Jewish, and 170 people had been criminally charged over the riots, of whom 155 were Arab and 15 Jewish. On 23 May, it was reported that 10% of those arrested over the riots were Jews, with the vast majority of those arrested being Arabs. On 24 May, the police launched a sweeping operation to arrest rioters called Operation Law and Order, deploying thousands of police officers to carry out mass arrests of suspected rioters. By 25 May, over 1,550 people had been arrested. On 3 June, the police announced the completion of arrests, of 2,142 arrested, 91% were Arab. As of May 2022, around 90% of 600 people indicted are Arabs.

According to Amnesty International, most of the arrests of Israeli-Arabs were for "insulting or assaulting a police officer" or "taking part in an illegal gathering" while right-wing Jewish extremists were mainly able to organize freely. The organization claimed that a "catalogue of violations" was committed by Israeli police against Palestinians in Israel and occupied East Jerusalem. "On at least two occasions in Haifa and Nazareth, witness accounts and verified videos showed police attacking groups of unarmed protesters without provocation", Amnesty reported.

Hamas delivered an ultimatum to Israel to remove all its police and military personnel from both the Haram al Sharif mosque site and Sheikh Jarrah by 10 May 6 p.m. If it failed to do so, they announced that the combined militias of the Gaza Strip ("joint operations room") would strike Israel. Minutes after the deadline passed, Hamas fired more than 150 rockets into Israel from Gaza. The Israel Defense Forces (IDF) said that seven rockets were fired toward Jerusalem and Beit Shemesh and that one was intercepted. An anti-tank missile was also fired at an Israeli civilian vehicle, injuring the driver. Israel launched air strikes in the Gaza Strip on the same day. Hamas called the ensuing conflict the "Sword of Jerusalem Battle." The following day, the IDF officially dubbed the campaign in the Gaza Strip "Operation Guardian of the Walls."

On 11 May, Hamas and Palestinian Islamic Jihad launched hundreds of rockets at Ashdod and Ashkelon, killing two people and wounding more than 90 others. A third Israeli woman from Rishon LeZion was also killed, while two more civilians from Dahmash were killed by a rocket attack. On 11 May, the 13-story residential Hanadi Tower in Gaza collapsed after being hit by an Israeli airstrike. The tower housed a mix of residential apartments and commercial offices. IDF said the building contained offices used by Hamas, and said it gave "advance warning to civilians in the building and provided sufficient time for them to evacuate the site"; Hamas and Palestinian Islamic Jihad fired 137 rockets at Tel Aviv in five minutes. Hamas stated that they fired their "largest ever barrage." In addition, an Israeli state-owned oil pipeline was hit by a rocket. On 12 May, Israeli Air Force destroyed dozens of police and security installations along the Gaza Strip; Hamas said its police headquarters were among the targets destroyed. Over 850 rockets were launched from Gaza into Israel on 12 May. According to the IDF, at least 200 rockets launched by Hamas failed to reach Israel, and fell inside the Gaza Strip. Hamas also struck an Israeli military jeep near the Gaza border with an anti-tank missile. An Israeli soldier was killed and three others were wounded in the attack.

On 13 May, Israeli forces and militant groups in Gaza continued to exchange artillery fire and airstrikes. Hamas attempted to deploy suicide drones against Israeli targets, with an Israeli F-16 engaging and shooting down one such drone. The Iron Dome intercepted many of the rockets fired at Israel. A series of Israeli strikes targeted the headquarters of Hamas' internal security forces, its central bank, and the home of a senior Hamas commander. On 14 May, Israel Defense Forces claimed to have troops on the ground and in the air attacking the Gaza Strip, although this claim was later retracted and followed with an apology for misleading the press. Israeli troops were reportedly told that they would be sent into Gaza and ground forces were reportedly positioned along the border as though they were preparing to launch an invasion. That same day, the Israeli Air Force launched a massive bombardment of Hamas' extensive underground tunnel network, which was known as "the metro", as well as above-ground positions, reportedly inflicting heavy casualties.

It was suspected that the reports of an Israeli ground invasion had been a deliberate ruse to lure Hamas operatives into the tunnels and prepared positions above ground to confront Israeli ground forces so that large numbers could then be killed by airstrikes. According to an Israeli official, the attacks killed hundreds of Hamas personnel, and in addition, 20 Hamas commanders were assassinated and most of its rocket production capabilities were destroyed. However, the estimated Hamas death toll was revised to dozens, as information came out that senior Hamas commanders had doubted that the ruse was genuine and only a few dozen Hamas fighters took positions in the tunnels. In total, 160 Israeli Air Force aircraft fired 450 missiles at 150 targets, with the attacks lasting about 40 minutes.[197][198] Also on 14 May, a Hamas drone was downed by Israeli air defense forces.

Chapter 11
No place for reformer in Islam

Musaylima, also known as Maslama ibn Ḥabīb was a preacher of monotheism from the Banu Hanifa tribe in 7th century Arabia. He claimed to be a prophet in 7th century Arabia. He was a leader during the Ridda wars. But Muslims labeled him a false prophet. Musaylima was the son of Habib, of the tribe Banu Hanifa, one of the largest tribes of Arabia that inhabited the region of Najd. The Banu Hanifa were a Hanafite Christian branch of Banu Bakr and led an independent existence prior to Islam. Among the first records of him is in late 9th Hijri, the Year of Delegations, when he accompanied a delegation of his tribe to Medina. The delegation included two other prominent Muslims.

They would later help Musaylima rise to power and save their tribe from destruction. These men were Nahar Ar-Rajjal bin Unfuwa and Muja'a bin Marara. In Medina, the deputation stayed with the daughter of al-Harith, a woman of the Ansar from the Banu Najjar. When the delegation arrived at Medina the camels were tied in a traveler's camp, and Musaylima remained there to look after them while the other delegates went in. They had talks with Muhammad. The delegation before their departure embraced Islam and renounced Christianity without compunction. As was his custom, Muhammad presented gifts to the delegates, and when they had received their gifts one said, "We left one of our comrades in the camp to look after our mounts."

Musaylima shared verses which he received from God. Musaylima taught 3 daily prayers to God, facing any direction. He criticized Muslims for selecting the Kaaba as the direction of prayers, arguing that God is not limited to one direction. He declared that the Kaaba was not the House of God, because an all-powerful God has no house. Musaylima said fasting should be at night instead of daytime during Ramadan. He prohibited circumcision. He considered men and women equal, and allowed premarital sex. He prohibited polygamy and cousin marriage. He declared that any slave who converted to his religion would become free. Musaylima stated that Iblis did not exist, because a fair and merciful God would not allow a being like Iblis to throw people into error. He also said it was wrong to include his name or any prophet's name in worship to God.

Musaylima shared verses purporting them to have been revelations from God. Thereafter, some of the people accepted him as a prophet alongside Muhammad. Gradually the influence and authority of Musaylima increased with the people of his tribe. He gathered an army of 40,000 followers. He also took to addressing gatherings as a messenger of Allah just like Muhammad, and would compose verses and offer them, as Quranic revelations.

During the Ridda wars which emerged following the death of Muhammad, Sajah bint al-Harith declared that she was a prophetess after learning that Musaylima and Tulayha had declared prophethood. 4,000 people gathered around her to march on Medina. Others joined her against Medina. However, her planned attack on Medina was called off after she learned that the army of Khalid ibn al-Walid had defeated Tulayha al-Asadi (another self-proclaimed prophet). Thereafter, she sought cooperation with Musaylima to oppose the threat of Khalid. A mutual understanding was initially reached with Musaylima. Later, the two married and she accepted his self-declared prophethood. Khalid then defeated the remaining rebellious elements around Sajah, and then moved on to defeat Musaylima. Musaylima fought and was killed in the Battle of Yamama.

Musaylima's followers survived at least till the 17th century. At the Mughal ruler Akbar's council of religions, a discussion of Musaylima religion also took place with the help of its priests. His teachings were almost lost but a neutral review of them does exist in Dabestan-e Mazaheb. Muslim writers often portray Musaylima negatively. But he gives a fascinating picture into 7th century Arabia where religious reformations were taking place and people were eager to accept new ideas, including that of Muhammad and his contemporary Musaylima. Musaylima claimed he received numerous revelations from God just like Muhammad did. Musaylima gathered an army of 40,000 followers.

Musaylima, who is alleged as having been a skilled magician by Muslim historians, dazzled the crowd with miracles. He could put an egg in a bottle; he could cut off the feathers of a bird and then stick them on so the bird would fly again; and he used this skill to persuade the people that he was divinely gifted.

Mansour al-Hallaj

Mansour al-Hallaj was a Persian mystic born in 858 CE in Iran. He is celebrated for his sacrifice towards worship. He was executed for staying firm on his spiritual Path. He died in 922 CE in Iraq. Mansur al-Hallaj was born in 858 CE in the Fars Province of Iran. He is best known for his saying: "I am the Truth" (Ana'l-Ḥaqq), which many saw as a claim to divinity, while others interpreted it as an instance of annihilation of the ego, allowing God to speak through him. Al-Hallaj gained a wide following as a preacher before he became implicated in power struggles of the Abbasid court and was executed after a long period of confinement on religious and political charges. Although most of his Sufi contemporaries disapproved of his actions, Hallaj later became a major figure in the Sufi tradition.

Al-Hallaj was born around 858 in Fars province of Persia to a cotton-carder (Hallaj means "cotton-carder" in Arabic) in an Arabized town called al-Bayḍā'. His grandfather was a Zoroastrian magi. His father moved to a town in Wasit famous for its school of Quran reciters. Al-Hallaj memorized the Quran before he was 12 years old and would often retreat from worldly pursuits to join other mystics in study at the school of Sahl al-Tustari. During this period Al-Hallaj lost his ability to speak Persian and later wrote exclusively in Arabic. Al Hallaj was a Sunni Muslim.

When he was twenty, al-Hallaj moved to Basra, where he married and received his Sufi habit from 'Amr Makkī, although his lifelong and monogamous marriage later provoked jealousy and opposition from the latter. Through his brother-in-law, al-Hallaj found himself in contact with a clan which supported the Zaydi Zanj rebellion, which had elements of Shi'i school of thought. He later went to Baghdad to consult the famous Sufi teacher Junayd Baghdadi, but he was tired of the conflict that existed between his father-in-law and 'Amr Makkī and he set out on a pilgrimage to Mecca, against the advice of Junayd Baghdadi, as soon as the Zanj rebellion was crushed.

In Mecca he made a vow to remain for one year in the courtyard of the sanctuary in fasting and total silence. When he returned from Mecca, he laid down the Sufi tunic and adopted a "lay habit" in order to be able to preach more freely. At that time a number of Sunnis, including former Christians who would later become viziers at the Abbasid court, became his disciples, but other Sufis were scandalized, while some Mu'tazilis and Shias who held high posts in the government accused him of deception and incited the mob against him. Al-Hallaj left for eastern Iran and remained there for five years, preaching in the Arab colonies and fortified monasteries that housed volunteer fighters in the jihad, after which he was able to return and install his family in Baghdad.

Al-Hallaj made his second pilgrimage to Mecca with four hundred disciples, where some Sufis, his former friends, accused him of sorcery and making a pact with the jinn. Afterwards he set out on a long voyage that took him to India and Turkestan beyond the frontiers of Islamic lands. About 290/902 he returned to Mecca for his final pilgrimage clad in an Indian loin-cloth and a patched garment over his shoulders. There he prayed to God to be made despised and rejected, so that God alone might grant grace to Himself through His servant's lips.

After returning to his family in Baghdad, al-Hallaj began making proclamations that aroused popular emotion and caused anxiety among the educated classes. These included avowing his burning love of God and his desire to "die accursed for the Community", and statements such as "O Muslims, save me from God, God has made my blood lawful to you: kill me". It was at that time that al-Hallaj is said to have pronounced his famous utterance "I am the Truth". He was denounced at the court, but a Shafi'i jurist refused to condemn him, stating that spiritual inspiration was beyond his jurisdiction. Al-Hallaj's preaching had by now inspired a movement for moral and political reform in Baghdad. In 296/908 Sunni reformers made an unsuccessful attempt to depose the underage caliph Al-Muqtadir. When he was restored, his Shi'i vizier unleashed anti-Hanbali repressions which prompted al-Hallaj to flee Baghdad, but three years later he was arrested, brought back, and put in prison, where he remained for nine years.

The conditions of Al-Hallaj's confinement varied depending on the relative sway his opponents and supporters held at the court, but he was finally condemned to death in 922 on the charge of being a Qarmatian rebel who wished to destroy the Kaaba, because he had said "the important thing is to proceed seven times around the Kaaba of one's heart." According to another report, the pretext was his recommendation to build local replicas of the Kaaba for those who are unable to make the pilgrimage to Mecca. The queen-mother interceded with the caliph who initially revoked the execution order, but the intrigues of the vizier finally moved him to approve it.

On 25 March trumpets announced his execution the next day. The words he spoke during the last night in his cell are collected in Akhbar al-Hallaj. Thousands of people witnessed his execution on the banks of the Tigris River. He was first punched in the face by his executioner, then lashed until unconscious, and then hanged. Witnesses reported that Al-Hallaj's last words under torture were "all that matters for the ecstatic is that the Unique should reduce him to Unity", after which he recited the Quranic verse 42:18. His body was doused in oil and set alight, and his ashes were then scattered into the river. A cenotaph was "quickly" built on the site of his execution, and "drew pilgrims for a millennium" until being swept away by a Tigris flood during the 1920s.

Some question whether al-Hallaj was executed for religious reasons as has been commonly assumed. According to Carl W. Ernst, the legal notion of blasphemy was not clearly defined in Islamic law and statements of this kind were treated inconsistently by legal authorities. In practice, since apostasy was subsumed under the category of zandaqa, which reflected the Zoroastrian legacy of viewing heresy as a political crime, they were prosecuted only when it was politically convenient. Sadakat Kadri points out that "it was far from conventional to punish heresy in the tenth century," and it is thought he would have been spared execution except that the vizier of Caliph Al-Muqtadir wished to discredit "certain figures who had associated themselves" with al-Hallaj.

Al-Hallaj addressed himself to popular audiences encouraging them to find God inside their own souls, which earned him the title of "the carder of innermost souls". He preached without the traditional Sufi habit and used language familiar to the local Shi'i population. This may have given the impression that he was a Qarmatian missionary rather than a Sufi. His prayer to God to make him lost and despised can be regarded as typical for a Sufi seeking annihilation in God, although Louis Massignon has interpreted it as an expression of a desire to sacrifice himself as atonement on behalf of all Muslims. When al-Hallaj returned to Baghdad from his last pilgrimage to Mecca, he built a model of the Kaaba in his home for private worship.

Al-Hallaj was popularly credited with numerous supernatural acts. He was said to have "lit four hundred oil lamps in Jerusalem's Church of the Holy Sepulchre with his finger and extinguished an eternal Zoroastrian flame with the tug of a sleeve." Among other Sufis, Al-Hallaj was an anomaly. Many Sufi masters felt that it was inappropriate to share mysticism with the masses, yet Al-Hallaj openly did so in his writings and through his teachings. This was exacerbated by occasions when he would fall into trances which he attributed to being in the presence of God. Hallaj was also accused of incarnationism, the basis of which charge seems to be a disputed verse in which the author proclaims mystical union in terms of two spirits in one body. There are conflicting reports about his most famous utterance "I am The Truth," which was taken to mean that he was claiming to be God.

The earliest report, coming from a hostile account of Basra grammarians, states that he said it in the mosque of Al-Mansur, while testimonies that emerged decades later claimed that it was said in private during consultations with Junayd Baghdadi. Even though this utterance has become inseparably associated with his execution in the popular imagination, owing in part to its inclusion in his biography by Attar of Nishapur, the historical issues surrounding his execution are far more complex.

Chapter 12
The Bahaism Faith

Bahaullah (1817–1892) was the prophet-founder of the Bahá'í Faith (Bahaism). He was born to an aristocratic family in Iran, and was exiled due to his adherence to the messianic Bahaism faith. In 1863, in Iraq, he first announced his claim to a revelation from God, and spent the rest of his life in further imprisonment in the Ottoman Empire. His teachings revolved around the principles of unity and religious renewal, ranging from moral and spiritual progress to world governance.

If we look at Bahaullah's life, it is true that was raised with no formal education but was well read and devoutly religious. One of the plus points with him was that his family was considerably wealthy, and at the age of 22 he turned down a position in the government, instead managing family properties and donating considerable time and money to charities. At the age of 27 he accepted the claim of the Báb and became among the most outspoken supporters of the new religious movement that advocated, among other things, abrogation of Islamic law, which attracted heavy opposition. At the age of 33, during an attempt to exterminate the movement, Bahaullah narrowly escaped death, his properties were confiscated, and he was banished from Iran.

Just before leaving, while imprisoned in a foul dungeon, Bahaullah claimed to receive revelations from God marking the beginning of his divine mission. After settling in Iraq, he again attracted the ire of Iranian authorities, and they requested that the Ottoman government move him farther away. He spent months in Istanbul where the authorities became hostile to his religious claims and put him in house arrest in Edirne for four years, followed by a harsh confinement in the prison of 'Akká, where he spent his final 24 years. Bahaullah wrote at least 1,500 letters, some of them book-length, that have been translated into at least 802 languages. Some notable examples include The Hidden Words, the Book of Certitude, and the Kitáb-i-Aqdas. Some teachings are mystical and address the nature of God and the progress of the soul, while others address the needs of society, religious obligations of his followers, or the structure of Bahá'í institutions that would propagate the religion. He viewed humans as fundamentally spiritual beings, and called upon individuals to develop divine virtues and further the material and spiritual advancement of human society.

Bahaullah died in 1892 near 'Akká. His burial place is a destination for pilgrimage by his followers, known as Bahá'ís, who now reside in 236 countries and territories, number between 5 and 8 million, and represent the only independent world religion to emerge in the modern age. Bahá'ís regard Bahaullah as a messenger or manifestation of God in succession to Buddha, Jesus, or Muhammad. The Bahaism faith is a relatively new religion teaching the essential worth of all religions and the unity of all people. Established by Bahaullah in the 19th century, it initially developed in Iran and parts of the Middle East, where it has faced ongoing persecution since its inception. The religion is estimated to have 5–8 million adherents, known as Bahá'ís, spread throughout most of the world's countries and territories.

The Bahaism faith has three central figures in its religious circle: the Báb (1819–1850), considered a herald who taught his followers that God would soon send a prophet similar to Jesus or Muhammad, and was executed by Iranian authorities in 1850; Bahaullah (1817–1892), who claimed to be that prophet in 1863 and faced exile and imprisonment for most of his life; and his son, 'Abdu'l-Bahá (1844–1921), who was released from confinement in 1908 and made teaching trips to Europe and the United States. After 'Abdu'l-Bahá's death in 1921, the leadership of the religion fell to his grandson Shoghi Effendi (1897–1957). Bahá'ís annually elect local, regional, and national Spiritual Assemblies that govern the religion's affairs, and every five years an election is held for the Universal House of Justice, the nine-member supreme governing institution of the worldwide Bahá'í community that is located in Haifa, Israel, near the Shrine of the Báb.

According to Bahaist teachings, religion is revealed in an orderly and progressive way by a single God through Manifestations of God, who are the founders of major world religions throughout history; Buddha, Jesus, and Muhammad are noted as the most recent of these before the Báb and Bahaullah. Bahá'ís regard the world's major religions as fundamentally unified in purpose, though varied in social practices and interpretations. The Bahá'í Faith stresses the unity of all people, explicitly rejecting racism, sexism, and nationalism. At the heart of Bahá'í teachings is the goal of a unified world order that ensures the prosperity of all nations, races, creeds, and classes.

The teachings of Bahaullah form the foundation of Bahá'í belief. Three principles are central to these teachings: the unity of God, the unity of religion, and the unity of humanity.[18] Baha'is believe that God periodically reveals his will through divine messengers, whose purpose is to transform the character of humankind and to develop, within those who respond, moral and spiritual qualities. Religion is thus seen as orderly, unified, and progressive from age to age. The Bahá'í writings describe a single, personal, inaccessible, omniscient, omnipresent, imperishable, and almighty God who is the creator of all things in the universe. The existence of God and the universe is thought to be eternal, without a beginning or end. Though inaccessible directly, God is nevertheless seen as conscious of creation, with a will and purpose expressed through messengers called Manifestations of God.

Bahá'í teachings state that God is too great for humans to fully comprehend, or to create a complete and accurate image of by themselves. Therefore, human understanding of God is achieved through his revelations via his Manifestations. In the Bahá'í Faith, God is often referred to by titles and attributes (for example, the All-Powerful, or the All-Loving), and there is a substantial emphasis on monotheism. Bahá'í teachings state that the attributes applied to God are used to translate Godliness into human terms and to help people concentrate on their own attributes in worshipping God to develop their potentialities on their spiritual path. According to the Bahá'í teachings the human purpose is to learn to know and love God through such methods as prayer, reflection, and being of service to others.

Bahá'í notions of progressive religious revelation result in their accepting the validity of the well-known religions of the world, whose founders and central figures are seen as Manifestations of God. Religious history is interpreted as a series of dispensations, where each manifestation brings a somewhat broader and more advanced revelation that is rendered as a text of scripture and passed on through history with greater or lesser reliability but at least true in substance, suited for the time and place in which it was expressed. Specific religious social teachings may be revoked by a subsequent manifestation so that a more appropriate requirement for the time and place may be established. Conversely, certain general principles (for example, neighborliness, or charity) are seen to be universal and consistent. In Bahá'í belief, this process of progressive revelation will not end; it is, however, believed to be cyclical. Bahá'ís do not expect a new manifestation of God to appear within 1000 years of Bahaullah's revelation.

Bahá'ís assert that their religion is a distinct tradition with its own scriptures and laws, and not a sect of another religion. The religion was initially seen as a sect of Islam because of its origins. Most religious specialists now see it as an independent religion, with its religious background in Shi'a Islam being seen as analogous to the Jewish context in which Christianity was established. Bahá'ís describe their faith as an independent world religion, differing from the other traditions in its relative age and in the appropriateness of Bahaullah's teachings to the modern context. He is believed to have fulfilled the messianic expectations of these precursor faiths.

The Bahá'í writings state that human beings have a "rational soul", and that this provides the species with a unique capacity to recognize God's status and humanity's relationship with its creator. Every human is seen to have a duty to recognize God through his Messengers, and to conform to their teachings. Through recognition and obedience, service to humanity and regular prayer and spiritual practice, the Bahá'í writings state that the soul becomes closer to God, the spiritual ideal in Bahá'í belief. According to Bahá'í belief when a human dies the soul is permanently separated from the body and carries on in the next world where it is judged based on the person's actions in the physical world. Heaven and Hell are taught to be spiritual states of nearness or distance from God that describe relationships in this world and the next, and not physical places of reward and punishment achieved after death.

The Bahá'í writings emphasize the essential equality of human beings, and the abolition of prejudice. Humanity is seen as essentially one, though highly varied; its diversity of race and culture are seen as worthy of appreciation and acceptance. Doctrines of racism, nationalism, caste, social class, and gender-based hierarchy are seen as artificial impediments to unity. The Bahá'í teachings state that the unification of humanity is the paramount issue in the religious and political conditions of the present world.

Cromosys Publication

The Plundering Prophet

Niranjan Jha Showman

The End

NIRANJAN JHA SHOWMAN

Cromosys Publication
Teach
Yourself
German
NIRANJAN JHA SHOWMAN

Cromosys Publication
Teach Yourself French
NIRANJAN JHA SHOWMAN

Cromosys Publication
Teach
Yourself
Spanish
NIRANJAN JHA SHOWMAN

Cromosys Publication

English
Voice
Accent and
Pronunciation

NIRANJAN JHA SHOWMAN

Teach Yourself Autodesk MAYA

Cromosys Publication

NIRANJAN JHA SHOWMAN

Cromosys Publication
Teach
Yourself
Autodesk
3ds Max
NIRANJAN JHA SHOWMAN

Cromosys Publication
CRIMINAL FACTORY
NIRANJAN JHA SHOWMAN

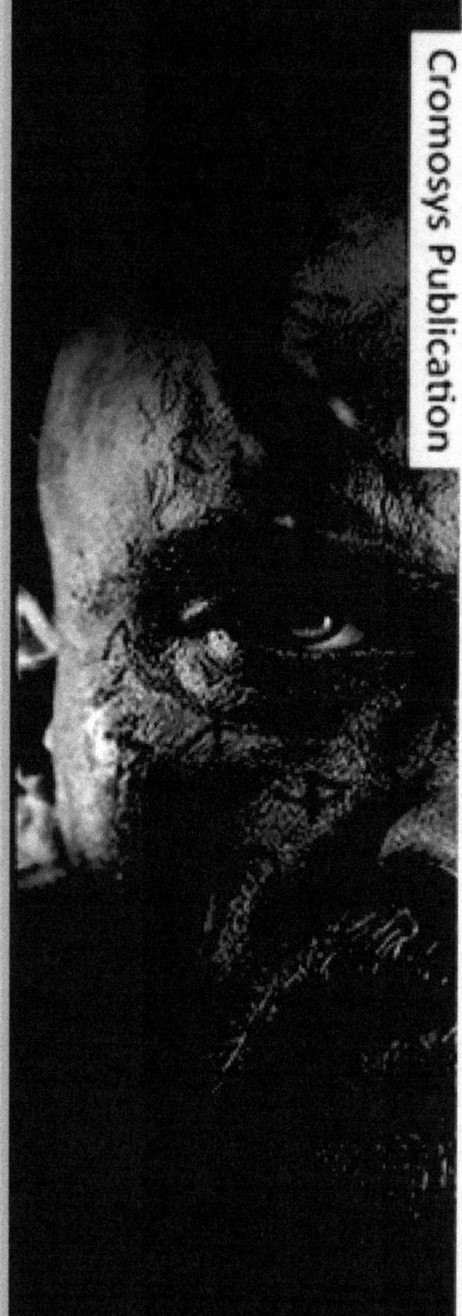

Cromosys Publication
FOCAL DISASTER
NIRANJAN JHA SHOWMAN

Cromosys Publication
Your talents will not help you succeed without your skill of using them.
NIRANJAN JHA SHOWMAN
BE
MILLIONAIRE
LIKE
ME

Read As Much As Possible